D1191105

An Ambassador's Guide

The BLUE BOOK *on* EVANGELISM

RAY COMFORT

Living Waters Publications
Bellflower, CA

The Blue Book on Evangelism
An Ambassador's Guide

Published by:
Living Waters Publications
P.O. Box 1172
Bellflower, CA 90706
www.livingwaters.com

Printed in the United States of America

ISBN 978-1-878859-46-4

Unless otherwise indicated, Scripture quotations are from the *New King James* version, ©1979, 1980, 1982 by Thomas Nelson Inc., Publishers, Nashville, Tennessee.

Scripture quotations designated KJV are from the *King James* version

Edited by Lynn Copeland

Cover, page design, and production by Genesis Group (www.genesis-group.net)

Photos by Carol Scott, Covina, CA (www.cj-studio.com)

CONTENTS

FOREWORD

I n the secular world, an ambassador is defined as a diplomat of the highest rank, accredited as a representative from one country to another. Every born-again follower of Jesus Christ is given the task of being an ambassador, an accredited representative of our great God and King. Such a priceless and undeserved honor is bestowed upon each of us the moment we step from the kingdom of Satan to the Kingdom of God.

The apostle Paul defines the responsibility of an ambassador: to implore people on behalf of Christ to be reconciled to God, by boldly proclaiming the gospel (2 Corinthians 5:20; Ephesians 6:19,20). Every true Christian must realize that he is first a representative of his Lord who saved him from the penalty of sin and God's just and holy wrath. Sadly, too few Christians fulfill their God-given mandate to represent their King as heralds of the message of the Kingdom of Heaven to a lost and dying world. They have forgotten that the gospel is a *spoken* message—one that requires a messenger to deliver (Romans 10:14–17).

This truth has not been lost on Ray Comfort. For decades, Ray has served as a faithful ambassador of Jesus Christ. He has preached the gospel in the open air quite literally around the world, reaching an untold number of people with the gospel of Jesus Christ. Over the years, Ray has encouraged and mentored many Christians to serve the King as one of His ambassadors. I am honored and blessed to be among them.

Ray Comfort is passionate about training other Christians to serve as ambassadors; and that passion and vision have resulted in the formation of the Ambassadors' Alliance and Ambassadors' Academy.

Over the years Ray has been asked many questions regarding his service to the King in proclaiming the gospel. *The Blue Book on Evangelism* is the result of some of that Q&A with other ambassadors. What you hold in your hands is more than a book. It is an ambassador's guide for serving the King, written by a faithful ambassador to faithful ambassadors.

I know you will be encouraged as you read *The Blue Book on Evangelism*. I have no doubt that you will refer to it often as you, an ambassador, bring the King's message to people who so desperately need to hear it.

TONY MIANO,
Director of the Ambassadors' Alliance

INTRODUCTION

Welcome to the Academy. We are glad you are here. I trust that it's your conviction that there is nothing more important than the salvation of the lost, and that you want to learn how you can be more effective in reaching them. I often liken evangelism to swimming. We can talk about it until we are blue in the faith, but if we don't dive in and do it, we will never swim. The Academy is about diving in.

I remember the first time I ever drove a car. I was terrified. I had to remember to do what seemed like a dozen things all at once. Steer straight. Watch the yellow line. Watch the rearview mirror. Keep your foot near the clutch. Be ready to brake. Watch for other cars. Be on the lookout for pedestrians. Watch for cyclists who may swerve. Keep an eye on your speed. Watch for the law. Don't tailgate, etc. However, after driving for too many years to remember, I could do it blindfolded. My problem now is that I could easily become overconfident, and that's not good when you are driving something that could kill people.

The same principles apply to evangelism. The first time you approach a stranger you will be terrified. So many things to remember. Be ready to stop and listen.

Use the Law. Watch for distractions. Head for the cross, etc. But after you do it again, then again, and again, your confidence will grow, and you will learn to steer the conversation anywhere you want. And if you will let love be your driving force, before you know it, evangelism will have become a way of life. Of course, you will have to battle fear continually to do it, but once you step out and witness, you will be so confident that no atheist, evolutionist, intellectual, agnostic, gnostic, or even caustic person, will intimidate you. Your only problem will be overconfidence. You will have to keep your heart free from pride, because that will hinder you, and we can't afford any hindrances when it comes to reaching out to the lost.

It is our earnest prayer that you leave a different person than when you came, and that you will turn your world upside down for the Kingdom of God.

May He bless you and yours, and give you your heart's desire.

Preparation

(Who & Why)

"Save some, O Christians!
By all means, save some. From yonder flames
and outer darkness, and the weeping, wailing,
and gnashing of teeth, seek to save some! Let
this, as in the case of the apostle, be your
great, ruling object in life, that by all means
you might save some."
—CHARLES SPURGEON

Question 1

I watched some of your open-air preaching and got a real sense of conviction. I was familiar with many of the principles you were teaching and my wife was involved in your ministries, but nothing ever clicked in me. I always thought that was for people older than me (I'm 20 years old), but after watching your videos I felt a certain dread come upon me that I really didn't even know if I would make it to an old age. A change has come upon me such as I have never felt before, and I can't listen to enough of your preaching or radio show or read enough of the Bible since then. Still, I struggle with having confidence to go in front of someone and share like you do. I just don't know if I know enough to go out and do that.

You can't use that as an excuse, because what is "enough"? All you need to know is the basics of the gospel. Never worry about some intellectual stumping you with a question you can't answer. You can always say, "I'm sorry. I don't know the answer to that." The truth is, you will never know how to do it, until you do it. So you must ignore your fears; they will leave the moment you begin. (I still have fear after all these years.) Start in the natural (maybe the death of a famous actor, or some news item, or trivia), swing to the fact that we will all die and be judged by the Commandments. Go through the Law, preach the cross, repentance, and faith. Then say, "Thank you for listening." Look on it as a learning experience at first. You are needed. People are going to Hell and the laborers are few.

Question 2

I know God wants me to share my faith, but I feel that if I don't, God doesn't love me and that I cannot maintain a relationship with Him. If we are saved by faith and not by works, why can't I have that relationship with God without witnessing?

This is an honest question. Here is the problem. We know that we are saved because the fruit of God's Spirit begin manifesting through us. God is love, therefore we should be filled with love, if we have been truly saved (see Romans 5:5). Think of this scenario. You are in Africa. A child is lying on the ground in front of you starving to death. You have food in your hand. You know God wants you to share the food with the dying child. So the question is, "Why can't I have a good relationship with God, without sharing the food?" You have to answer that yourself.

> "I would sooner bring one sinner to Jesus than unravel all the mysteries of the Word, for salvation is the thing we are to live for."
>
> —CHARLES SPURGEON

Question 3

I want so much to share my faith and testimony, to speak in churches and share God's Word in the evangelist field. However, I haven't written a book (yet) and my name isn't known. How can I do this?

Ask God to open doors for you, and in the meanwhile, busy yourself doing menial things. Be a servant. My first international invitation to speak came when I was painting a restroom at a church. The second came when I was pushing a stranger's car because it wouldn't start. That spoke volumes to me about God honoring us when we are servants. So wash feet.

Question 4

Why do Christians have so much fear and hardship proclaiming the truth, when the cults and other religions have no troubling proclaiming lies?

It's important to remember that we fight a spiritual battle. Whenever we approach someone with the gospel, we battle the spirit of fear. However, those in cults and other religions are not wrestling against demonic forces. There is no battle for them. Instead of fighting against the enemy, they are fighting for him. But they also have another incentive. Their public agenda is to spread what they believe is the truth, but their *motive* is one of self-advancement. They don't believe that they will enter the kingdom unless they add works to their faith, so that becomes a strong incentive and energizer. The Christian, however, has a nobler motive. We reach out to the lost because we love God and because we are deeply concerned (horrified) at the fate of the unsaved.

Question 5

As a married woman, am I supposed to zealously witness the way that Paul and the other apostles did? I am refer-

13

ring to scriptures like 1 Timothy 2:9–15 and 1 Peter 3:1–6. I do believe that the husband is the head of the wife.

Just don't get into a position where you are exercising authority over men. Dress modestly, obey your husband, and make sure that you share your faith whenever and wherever you can. If your husband's not a Christian, then be a prayer warrior, and give out tracts and witness as much as you can without offending him and harming your relationship.

Question 6

Thus far I'm alone in my efforts in biblical evangelism in my city. Other Christians say they appreciate what I'm doing by going out on the streets but think it's because I have a "gift" for evangelism. They say it's not their gift or calling so they'll just stay in their comfort zone and pray for me. They hide behind Ephesians 4:11: "He Himself gave some to be apostles, some prophets, some evangelists, and some pastors and teachers."

Point out to them that some are called to be evangelists "for the equipping of the *saints* for the work of ministry." All Christians (saints) are commanded to evangelize. We have a moral obligation to do so. How can any person who professes to love God have no concern that sinners are going to Hell? To encourage and equip other believers to step out of their comfort zones to reach the lost, you may want to invite some to study "The Way of the Master" Basic Training Course in your home or church. Pray that God would raise up laborers, and see what you can do to help.

Question 7

Is it wise to send new converts out into the battlefield before they are grounded in the Word and apologetics?

It is the best thing you can do for them. The woman at the well didn't go to a seminary before she testified of the Savior, and she brought a whole village to Him. After finding Christ, Andrew immediately told Simon Peter. The first thing Philip did was find Nathanael and immediately tell him about the Savior (see John chapter 1). If new converts came to Christ under the sound of the Law, they know enough to go and do likewise with the lost. They will make mistakes. They may get bruised. But that is how we learned to walk in this life, and the same is true spiritually.

Question 8

I got saved three years ago after listening to "Hell's Best Kept Secret" and since then have being bent on soul winning, but I've not been received well by my local church or really any-one in the Christian family (though I am by the lost). Still, I pray God gives me strength to push myself to witness in the steps of Christ. Do you have any advice?

You are not alone. There are many who find themselves almost isolated, simply because they are deeply burdened to reach the lost, and they want to do it biblically. That's one of the reasons we have the Ambassadors' Alliance, to encourage those who find themselves in such circumstances.

Question 9

How would you deal with a church staff and members who are not compassionate about soul winning or who do not believe in this type of winning the lost? Should I leave the church?

That, ultimately, has to be your decision. But I would add that you should hang in there as long as you can. Who knows what changes God could bring in your church through your prayers and perseverance. If you find yourself getting bitter or too frustrated, find another church that has a love for the unsaved. Ask God to give you wisdom so that you make the right decision, keeping in mind that you want a church to have a positive influence on your family.

Question 10

I have been a pastor for six years. God has given me the honor of leading a number of people to the Lord in my office when they come onto my turf for counsel. However, your show has inspired me to take the gospel to the streets. How can I overcome my fear of witnessing on the sinner's turf?

There are a number of ways to overcome fear. First, realize that it is spiritual. The Bible speaks of it as "the spirit of fear." You are going to have to fight it every time you step out of your comfort zone. So don't listen to the enemy. Instead, be prayerful, and let love for the unsaved swallow your fears. See yourself as a brave firefighter who beats back fear because he wants to rescue a child from the flames.

Question 11

What should I do to prepare myself for going out witnessing?

One way to keep yourself always prepared is to constantly think about the fate of the unsaved. Think of yourself as a person living in the heart of a terrible drought. You have been given a supply of food and water to share. So how do you prepare yourself? You make sure you have food at hand for when you see someone who is starving to death. Our "food" is the gospel. That's what we want to get into the heart of dying humanity. You can use gospel tracts to get their mouths open. So, here's a summary: 1) Be prayerful. 2) Carry tracts. 3) Go over the gospel in your mind until you know how to present it biblically in three minutes, or in thirty minutes.

Those who use the excuse that they don't know what to say are perhaps those referred to in Scripture as being "ashamed" of the gospel. They are usually those who have never studied to show themselves approved as "a worker who does not need to be ashamed" (2 Timothy 2:15). Don't let that be true of you.

Question 12

I sometimes seem to "offend" people when I share my faith. They say that I am "attacking" them. How can I effectively share the Good News without offending? I realize that Jesus offended a lot of people, and I'm not worried about the effect of Truth, but I would just like to be more effective for my Lord.

You are right about there being a natural offense with the gospel, but perhaps it could also be your tone. Are you an "intense" person? We're called to speak with gentleness and respect, so be sure tour attitude is one of humble compassion. Do you take a moment to build a bridge with an unsaved person before you swing to spiritual things? Do you use a little humor before you transition to the things of God? (Some of our tracts can do that for you, if you are not personally inclined that way.) Ask a close Christian friend to listen as you witness to someone and see what he thinks.

Question 13

I've been out on the street witnessing for about three years now, one-to-one, and I can't say confidently that I have seen anyone "saved." I've seen so many cry and appear convicted, but none of them have ever called me or written about how their new faith is going. So the question is: What do you do when you feel like you're not doing anything at all?

This is such a good question, because you are going to have people come up to you and say things like, "I led

169 people to this Lord last week, praise the Lord. All glory to Him for what He's doing!" And there you are, faithfully laboring away, and you haven't seen anyone come to the Lord.

More than likely, the main reason that you don't see "decisions" for Christ is that you fear God. And because of that healthy fear of the Lord, you don't want to lead a single soul into a false profession of faith. We know how easy it is to get decisions and impress people with numbers, but we also know better. It would be easy to say to those who have heard the gospel, "Do you know for sure that your name is written in Heaven? Would you like to have that knowledge? I could lead you in a sinner's prayer right now, so you can know that when you die you will go to Heaven. Would you like to pray?" God forbid that you and I would contribute to the numbers of tares that are sitting among the wheat in the contemporary church.

> "When preaching and private talk are not available, you need to have a tract ready... Get good striking tracts, or none at all. But a touching gospel tract may be the seed of eternal life. Therefore, do not go out without your tracts."
>
> —CHARLES SPURGEON

I preached the gospel for twelve years almost daily, and hardly saw a soul come to Christ. However, after I left New Zealand and came to the United States, I started to hear of ones surrendering to Christ who had listened to the gospel so long ago.

So here is the way to keep yourself encouraged. See yourself as sowing in tears, then read these verses over and over, until you are familiar with them and understand them:

> "And he who reaps receives wages, and gathers fruit for eternal life, that both he who sows and he who reaps may rejoice together. For in this the saying is true: 'One sows and another reaps.' I sent you to reap that for which you have not labored; others have labored, and you have entered into their labors." (John 4:36–38)

> Therefore, my beloved brethren, be steadfast, immovable, always abounding in the work of the Lord, knowing that your labor is not in vain in the Lord. (1 Corinthians 15:58)

Never be discouraged. Keep asking God that you may see fruit for your labors, but don't let seeing fruit now be your source of encouragement and motivation. Let it simply be the fact that God is faithful to watch over His Word. There's nothing wrong with the seed of the gospel and it's up to God to cause it to bring life, in His perfect timing. You will see fruit *in eternity*. That's were it counts.

Question 14

Our motive for sharing and reaching out to the lost must be the love of Jesus. If it is anything else, our motive will be exposed and we'll be ineffective. How can we be sure our hearts are in the right place before hitting the streets?

Ask God to search out our motives. However, I would add one thing. Even if your heart isn't in the right place (I'm not talking about sin, but that you are going because of a sense of guilt), you should still go. If you were rescued from a burning building by a fireman who left the firehouse because he felt guilty not coming to the fire, as far as you are concerned, his motive for rescuing you is a non-issue. He did it. That's all that matters. So don't get hung up on why you reach out to the lost, just do it, while there is still time. The quality is in the seed, not the sower.

Question 15

Can you describe your prayer life and what role that plays in your evangelism—that is, do you do any kind of prayer walking before evangelism, etc.?

For the last twenty-five years, I have gotten up most nights of the week (around midnight) to seek God in prayer. It hasn't been easy. The key is to go to bed early. When I get up to pray I wrap a blanket around me and pray for about thirty minutes. Then I write for a couple of hours, read the Word and go back to sleep. I always have a pen and paper beside me when I pray.

When we leave to do an open air, we pray for God's help and His care for us driving the freeways. Just before we get up to preach, we pray. Then, after the preaching, we pray for those who heard the Word that day.

Question 16

How do you specifically pray for the lost?

I pray almost daily that God would raise up laborers. That's what Jesus told us to do: "The harvest truly is great, but the laborers are few; therefore pray the Lord of the harvest to send out laborers into His harvest" (Luke 10:2). That's the key to reaching the lost—more true and faithful laborers.

Question 17

How do you keep yourself primed to reach the lost?

The Scriptures say, "But sanctify the Lord God in your hearts, and always be ready to give a defense to everyone who asks you a reason for the hope that is in you, with meekness and fear" (1 Peter 3:15). I thought that I was "always ready" to give an answer, but the other day I found that I wasn't.

I was riding my bike to work when I saw a gentleman walking on the sidewalk. As I rode past him I offered him a Ten Commandments coin and said, "Did you get one of these?" He grabbed it from my hand and said, "Hey! Thank you very much!" He didn't know what it was, but he was so enthusiastic I immediately wished I had stopped and engaged him in a conversation about

the things of God. All the way to work I was kicking myself for not stopping, and I spent some time thinking about the incident. I came to the conclusion that I was not "always ready."

I had a subconscious mentality of "hit and run." I needed to have a predetermined mindset to engage in a conversation, before I encountered anyone.

A few days later I was riding to work when I saw a teenager on a skateboard heading for me. Suddenly, he slipped and sent the skateboard flying onto a busy road. He quickly ran out and retrieved it, and jumped back onto the sidewalk. I said a friendly, "That's was close!" and followed with, "Here's a million dollars for you." He smiled, then I said, "It's a gospel tract. What do you think happens after someone dies? Do you think there's a Heaven?" There was no offense on his part. He said, "I'm not sure." "Do you think there's a Hell?" "Definitely." That reply was interesting. So we went through the Commandments, opening up their spiritual nature.

It turned out that he had lied, stolen, lusted, and blasphemed God's name. He became rather sober, and it concerned him that because of his sins he was heading for Hell. I then shared the good news that Jesus paid his fine and rose from the dead, and upon his repentance and faith in Jesus, God would grant him everlasting life. We shook hands. He went on his way, and I went on mine.

So if you are a chicken like me and you fight inner fears, do yourself a big favor. Deal with your fears in the prayer closet, and predetermine to be ready. Always.

GETTING STARTED

(When & Where)

"If you never have sleepless hours, if you never have weeping eyes, if your hearts never swell as if they would burst, you need not anticipate that you will be called zealous. You do not know the beginning of true zeal, for the foundation of Christian zeal lies in the heart. The heart must be heavy with grief and yet must beat high with holy ardor. The heart must be vehement in desire, panting continually for God's glory, or else we shall never attain to anything like the zeal which God would have us know."
—CHARLES SPURGEON

Question 18

When you started to witness, did you take baby steps like first getting comfortable handing out tracts then on to a bit more confrontational witnessing, . . . or did you take a giant "big boy" step and just start open-air preaching? What was the process you went through? Did you have someone there to mentor you?

Yes, I did take baby steps, and I did fall over and get bruised. However, right from the moment of my conversion I was giving out tracts. If that's considered baby steps, I'm still taking them. Rather than using the baby analogy, I would rather liken evangelism to swimming. My flesh still hates diving into a swimming pool. The moment I do so it is very uncomfortable, but my flesh adjusts in seconds. It's the same with witnessing and open-air preaching—you have to will yourself to do it. Just do it. Dive in. It will make you grow like nothing else. No, I didn't have any mentor. My conscience was my coach. It drove me to do it.

The first time I open-air preached in the U.S. was off a trash bin at Waikiki in Hawaii. Shortly after that I wandered among the sunbathers and said, "Hello, folks. My name is Ray. It must be a dream to lie on this famous beach and enjoy the warmth of the Hawaiian sun . . . and it would probably be a nightmare for a preacher to suddenly stand up and preach to you. But I have something extremely important to tell you, and I will be as quick as I can." I preached for about twenty minutes before a police officer approached me and said, "I have had eight complaints. You had better wind down." He was a Christian, so he patiently waited as long as he could, to give me more time to share the gospel.

Question 19

Is it best to go out as Jesus sent the apostles, by twos?

You can, but it's not a rule. It seems that Paul preached by himself (such as on Mars Hill). There is no mention of Stephen having a team or a partner. I've preached by myself for many years. If you're open-air preaching, sometimes it's easier to go by yourself, so if you have a hard time at least you don't embarrass yourself in front of your friends. But if you're just getting your feet wet in witnessing, it's often helpful to go with a friend so you can encourage one another.

Question 20

My friend and I go to the local mall to witness for a few hours every week. Is it better to give out tracts to a lot of people, or to talk to only a few people but in more depth?

"Soul winning... should be the main pursuit of every true believer. We should each say with Simon Peter, 'I go a fishing,' and with Paul our aim should be, 'That I might by all means save some.'"
—CHARLES SPURGEON

Both are good. However, if I was to choose only one approach I would lean toward one-to-one. Jesus went out of His way to talk one-to-one with the woman at the well (John chapter 4). He could have spent His valuable time preaching to multitudes, but He used it to speak to her personally, and alone. The problem is that we have a lack of laborers. I know of some people who find one-to-one difficult, but they can pass out tracts like a machine. These are the type of laborers you and you friend should take with you so your nets can be cast further.

Question 21

What do you do if you live in a smaller town where there are only a few people at a time who walk down the street?

That's a difficult place to open-air preach. It may be best to hand out tracts and concentrate on witnessing one-to-one, or one-to-two. Make sure that you are rich in good works. Perhaps in winter you could stand somewhere giving out tracts with free hot chocolate, or with cool drinks in summer. Be sure to take advantage of any gatherings such as parades, citywide picnics, football games, etc., as well as county fairs and events in nearby cities. Even if these events are not conducive to open-air preaching, they're wonderful opportunities to give out plenty of tracts and witness one-to-one.

Question 22

Do you go to certain planned events, such as air shows, parades, etc., or do you stay away because you are competing with them?

Any gatherings like parades and air shows are perfect for giving out tracts, especially our Giant Money tract. These tracts are so large that each person who gets one becomes a walking advertisement for them, and you will soon have people approach you and say, "So you're the one giving out those big $100 bills. May I have one?"

Question 23

At public events, how do you witness to people individually? I've been to fairs, concerts, and downtown celebrations to witness and everybody there is with friends. I have witnessed to groups, but I think it's more effective one-to-one. What do you say when you approach a couple or a group of adults?

As you approach a group of two or more people and begin talking, often one person will be more friendly and responsive to you. To talk one-to-one, I simply address that person directly. It takes boldness to do this, but it seems to work, without offense. I say, "Let him speak. I want to know what he has to say." Often the rest of the group will get the hint and leave me to it. Speaking with a cooperative, interested person will allow you to share the gospel more effectively, while his companions can listen in.

Question 24

How can I set up a debate against an atheist at our local college campus? I have watched you do it and it is wonderful how you preach Christ and don't stray once.

Check out the college website and see if you can find any atheist or evolution group, and challenge them to a debate. Make it worth their while by offering them $100 for their time. All they have to do is give their evidence as to why God doesn't exist, and you will give evidence as to why He does. Let the audience decide. Ask a Christian group on campus to promote it. You may even get the atheists to promote it also. They will want it to be a success.

Question 25

We go into a youth detention center to minister once a month, and the staff restricts our message so we can't mention Hell, homosexuality, or sin in general. Even though I have pushed the limits a few times, I'm careful to try to stay within their guidelines. How would you handle this situation?

Perhaps you could fill your message with analogies—about a criminal having his "fine" paid by a loving judge, etc. Maybe you could give them applicable verses by saying, "Here is this month's memory verse," and offer a free Bible to those who recite the verse(s) correctly the next time.

THE WAY OF THE MASTER METHOD

(What)

"Lower the Law and you dim the light by which man perceives his guilt; this is a very serious loss to the sinner rather than a gain; for it lessens the likelihood of his conviction and conversion. I say you have deprived the gospel of its ablest auxiliary [its most powerful weapon] when you have set aside the Law. You have taken away from it the schoolmaster that is to bring men to Christ."

—CHARLES SPURGEON

Question 26

The message preached as the basis for "The Way of the Master" seems to be this: "Believe in Jesus and go to Heaven, because you don't want to go to Hell." I think that this philosophy, while true literally, misses the true concept that is found in Scripture. The reason to be a Christian and to serve God is not because "your skin will be singed," as Reidhead wrote. Rather it is because the Lord is worthy of all glory. We deserve Hell yet He has been merciful to us. The problem with salvation because of destination is that the person has no idea of the magnitude of his crimes.

The unregenerate human heart is so desperately wicked, the motive for fleeing from wrath should be honorable, but it's not. How could it be? The wicked criminal comes to be "saved" because he is wicked. How can a vile sinner suddenly become virtuous in motive? It would be admirable to have heard about the terrors of Hell and not been fearful, and instead have come to Christ because God is worthy of glory, but from where would a blind and lost sinner have found such theology? The truth is that there is nothing good in his own unregenerate and evil heart.

That is the reason we preach the Law—to show the sinner the magnitude of his crimes. Recognizing that he rightly deserves Hell—but is offered mercy instead—is what makes him respond in gratitude for all that Christ has done for him. Sinai produces fear of God, because of His wrath. Calvary produces love for God, because of His mercy.

Question 27

What scriptural proof can you offer that the way you witness to people is the way that Jesus witnessed? After all, you ask, "What *did* Jesus do?" and not "What *would* Jesus do?" So, please prove to me that your evangelism techniques are Jesus' evangelism techniques.

One example is in Mark 10, where the rich young ruler approached Jesus and asked what he should do to get everlasting life. Jesus first reproved the man's understanding of the word "good," then He showed him God's standards by going through five of the Ten Commandments. We have written an entire book called *What Did Jesus Do?* in answer to that question.

Question 28

Even though I believe your witnessing style is very effective and truly the way Christ approached sharing the gospel, I sometimes think you believe that born-again Christians aren't going to Heaven unless they come to Christ via the Ten Commandments. Is that true?

All born-again Christians are of course going to Heaven. For someone to come to Christ and be born again, he must repent. To repent, there must be knowledge of sin, and Paul said, "I would not have known sin except through the Law." All sin traces itself back to the Law, for "sin is transgression of the Law" (1 John 3:4, KJV). So I think the question is unfairly stated. It should rather be, is the principle that you teach biblical? If it isn't, drop it. If it is, embrace it with both hands.

Question 29

Using the Law and the prophets are definitely the necessary tools for reaching the proud. The Way of the Master has emphasized the prophets in a few books, but I haven't seen much detail about prophecy in actual one-to-one witnessing or open-air preaching. Is it best not to get into Bible prophecy, as Peter did in Acts 2, to target the intellect for people who don't believe that the Bible is true?

Prophecy addresses the intellect. The Law addresses the conscience. I often speak about how the words of Jesus parallel history before it came into being, and how Matthew 24 and Luke 21 are proofs of the inspiration of Scripture. However, I am quick to move from there to the Law. That's where the rubber meets the road—the cross makes no sense without the knowledge of sin.

> "If people are to be saved by a message, it must contain at least some measure of knowledge. There must be light as well as fire."
> —CHARLES SPURGEON

Question 30

Why was the Law omitted in evangelism at the turn of the last century? What caused preachers to stop using it?

It's baffling why any army would leave its greatest weapon in the barracks, and go into the battle armed with a feather duster. This, however, has revealed the subtlety of the enemy, and reminds us to be tenacious in our use of the Law to bring the knowledge of sin.

Question 31

What do you mean by "modern evangelism"? The statement that modern evangelism isn't working is vague. Are you including the popular "Steps to Peace with God" and Dr. D. James Kennedy's "Evangelism Explosion" approaches to reaching lost people?

The phrase "modern evangelism" is a generalization for the traditional evangelistic methods that are used by the contemporary Church, but are unbiblical. The vagueness has been deliberate, because I don't want to criticize any ministry. Our motive is solely to reach the lost. I have the utmost admiration for the ministries you mentioned. However, when essential biblical principles have been omitted from any accepted and respected gospel presentation, we need to see what the Scriptures say on the subject and then align with the Word of God.

We may have the greatest admiration for a brilliant doctor, but if we know that he has made a mistake in a prescription by leaving out an essential ingredient, we have to set aside our admiration for the doctor, and think of the welfare of the patient. It is clearly evident that the "patient" is deathly sick (by the patient, I don't mean the true Church, but rather the false converts that sit within the church—the "tares among the wheat," of which our churches are full). In January 2006, Dr. Kennedy aired "Hell's Best Kept Secret." He aired it twice in a year, the second time on "The Best of Truths That Transform." He would not have done so if the teaching was unbiblical or if he felt threatened or offended by it.

Question 32

Isn't your approach a modern method as well?

May I respectfully say, "Test it against Scripture." Be a Berean with this. It is based on foundational 2,000-year-old biblical principles. The use of the Law to bring the knowledge of sin is rooted in Holy Scripture. It may seem new to those who don't understand its true function, but it is definitely not "modern." To get you started, read Psalm 19:7; Romans 2:15; 3:19,20; 7:7; Galatians 3:24; 1 Timothy 1:8,9; 1 John 3:4.

Question 33

When talking with pastors about the Way of the Master and having an evangelism team in the church, their common question is, "How successful are your evangelistic efforts?" Since we are not pushing for conversions, we don't have those numbers to give. Also, a majority of people we witness to are not from our hometown, so we'll never see them walk into our church. So what do we point to as evidence of our efforts? Today's seeker-friendly church keeps requesting, "Show me the numbers!"

I am always amazed at the results pointed to by modern evangelism. They report how many were saved under their preaching, but how did they get access to the Book of Life? Making a "decision," walking an aisle, or raising a hand don't indicate whether someone truly repents and trusts in the Savior. I have no idea how many God may have saved through my planting of seed. The fact that I have planted the good seed of the Word of God is evangelistic "success." The rest is up to God. Read 1 Corinthians 15:58 over and over. Never be discouraged. Your labor isn't in vain.

Question 34

In your opinion, what is the number one reason people don't want to use this method of evangelism, other than fear of rejection?

That is a mystery to me. Why would anyone want to fish with a net that is full of holes, when God has provided a perfect net to catch men? My only explanation is that there is a spiritual blindness. I have lost count of the number of people who've said that they heard the teaching a second time and then suddenly "got it"! It was as though a light switched on in their heads.

Question 35

If someone understands that these truths are biblical and approves of the method, but replies, "It's not for me," how should we respond? Is this the only biblical method?

The question is simply, "Is it biblical?" Did Jesus use it? Did the disciples use it? Did the early church use it? If so, there should be no argument. If it is indeed the God-given key to reaching the lost, why *wouldn't* we use it? For further reading on the biblical basis for this teaching, we have a book on this subject called *What Did Jesus Do?*

Question 36

How do you reason with Christians who love God, but believe it is wrong to discuss sin with unbelievers? I have a dear sister in Christ who believes that fear of eternal damnation does not lead one to a long-term relationship with God; she believes in focusing only on the love of God.

This philosophy makes no sense if you follow her line of reasoning. Jesus was confrontational. He talked about sin. He spoke to the woman at the well (John chapter 4) about the fact that she was committing adultery. Study Paul in Romans chapter 2, or the Books of James, Peter, or Jude. The cold, hard fact is that if people die in their sins they will end up in Hell forever. If we love them, we will work with the Holy Spirit to do everything we can to awaken them to their danger. The Bible says that they are enemies of God and under His wrath, so saying, "God loves you" will only confuse them. Unless they repent, they will perish, and they won't repent if

they think that they are morally good.

Another point is, how do you show sinners that God loves them? Do you point to their health or wealth? If that's the criteria, millionaires are more loved than most of us, and healthy people are more loved than those who are gravely ill. The only biblical way to convince sinners that God loves them is to point to the cross. In almost every place in Scripture where God's love is mentioned, it is in correlation to the cross: "In this is love, not that we loved God, but that He loved us and *sent His Son to be a propitiation for our sins*" (1 John 4:10). "For God so loved the world that *He gave His only begotten Son*" (John 3:16). "God demonstrates His own love toward us, in that while we were still sinners, *Christ died for us*" (Romans 5:8), etc.

Question 37

When I use the Law as I witness to people, I sometimes wonder if anyone has watched "The Way of the Master" and then when I go through the Commandments with them they will recognize the "technique." How can we avoid becoming "cookie cutter" evangelists each with the same technique?

It was never my intention to have people do exactly what I do when sharing the gospel. So, just follow the biblical principle of Law to the proud and grace to the humble and let your own personality and ingenuity come through when you witness. Don't be too concerned with people's criticisms; our praise should be from God, not from men. I have had people say, "I've seen this on television," but I find that more of a help than a hindrance.

Question 38

What if someone says they don't believe we'll be judged by the Ten Commandments?

The Bible makes it clear that there will be a Day of Judgment. The Scriptures warn, "Though they join forces, the wicked will not go unpunished" (Proverbs 11:21). However, there are those who question the standard of judgment—will it be the Ten Commandments, the moral Law? Some say that it will rather be the words of Jesus that will judge mankind. This belief is based on John 12:48: "He who rejects Me, and does not receive My words, has that which judges him—the word that I have spoken will judge him in the last day."

Humanity will be judged by the words of Jesus, but remember that the Scriptures say that the Lord would "magnify the law and make it honorable" (Isaiah 42:21, KJV). This was the essence of the teaching ministry of the Messiah. The religious leaders had twisted the Law and demeaned it so that its original intend was lost. But Jesus magnified it. He showed them that lust was adultery, and that anger without cause violated its holy precepts, etc. He reminded them that not one jot or tittle of the Law would fail.

When Paul preached on Mars Hill, he warned the idolatrous Athenians that God would judge the world "in righteousness." They had violated the First and Second of the Ten Commandments and he therefore warned them that God was not "shaped by art and man's devising." The "righteousness" of which he spoke is the righteousness which is of the Law: "For as many as have sinned without law will also perish without law, and as many as have sinned in the law *will be judged by the law*" (Romans 2:12, emphasis added). James 2:12 also warns that the moral Law will be the standard of judgment: "So speak and so do as those who will be judged by the law of liberty."

Those who may be tempted to say that the "law of liberty" isn't the moral Law but "the law of Christ" should look at the context. The preceding verse says: "For He who said, '*Do not commit adultery*' [7th Commandment], also said, '*Do not murder*' [8th Commandment]. Now if you do not commit adultery, but you do murder, you have become a transgressor of the law" (James 2:11).

Question 39

What about the role of your testimony in witnessing? Isn't it helpful to tell others what Christ has done in our own lives as part of our sharing?

Absolutely. If I remember rightly, the apostle Paul shared his personal testimony three times in the Book of Acts. Just make sure you weave the Law into your testimony. Too often we give the impression that we weren't happy, that there was something missing in our lives, until we found Jesus. Instead, explain how you came to see that

"God be thanked when the Law so works as to take off the sinner from all confidence in himself! To make the leper confess that he is incurable is going a great way toward compelling him to go to that divine Savior, who alone is able to heal him."
—CHARLES SPURGEON

you were condemned under the Law, headed for Hell, and how God's grace saved you through the cross, etc.

Question 40

Why is there so much opposition among evangelicals concerning the Way of the Master, whether in open-air or one-to-one, and how do we approach this?

It is spiritual, so make sure that you fight it spiritually, with prayer, love, and self-control.

HANDLING A WITNESSING ENCOUNTER

(How)

*"I have known what it is to use up all my
ammunition, and then I have, as it were,
rammed myself into the great gospel gun and
fired myself at the hearers—all my experience
of God's goodness, all my consciousness of sin,
and all my sense of the power of the gospel."*
—CHARLES SPURGEON

Question 41

What do you do when the person you're witnessing to tries to turn the conversation into a debate? A Catholic fellow who was very well versed in evangelical doctrine kept asking me what I believed about non-essential doctrines, and whether I knew that other evangelicals would disagree with me. If I didn't support a particular doctrine, he tried to debate me on it, even though he didn't believe it himself. I tried going through the Law with him, but we never got anywhere with it. We just ended up with a lengthy, friendly discussion on evangelical differences.

I would be firm with someone like this and say, "How about I give you two minutes to speak, without interruption, and then you give me two minutes." Make sure he agrees to do this, then hold him to his word and take him through the Commandments.

Question 42

What do you do when someone still doesn't see his sin, even after I took him through the Ten Commandments? I talked to one person who was convinced that lust really wasn't a violation of the Ten Commandments.

If a man rapes a woman and doesn't think that rape is a violation of man's law, it doesn't change the fact that it is. Here is proof that lust is a violation of the Ten Commandments: "You have heard that it was said to those of old, 'You shall not commit adultery' [Seventh Commandment]. But I say to you that whoever looks at a woman to lust for her has already committed adultery with her in his heart" (Matthew 5:27,28). So there you have it from the highest authority on earth—the Word of the Living God. If you have the word of a king or a president, you have it on great authority. But this comes from the authority of the Word of God Himself. So, make sure that you quote the verse and don't just refer to it. Jesus quoted the Old Testament word for word when He was tempted by the devil. God's Word doesn't return void. It is quick and powerful and cuts through to the marrow of a sinner's bones, so quote it when you share the gospel.

Another way to strengthen the lust argument is to reason about it. Tell the sinner that "lust" is pornography of the mind. Ask him if he thinks child porn okay. The odds are he will say that it's morally wrong. That's his moral standard. God's standard is higher than his, and He says that lust for anyone other than your spouse is morally wrong.

Also, never forget that you have the sinner's conscience on your side. It bears witness with the Law (see Romans 2:15), and of course you have the help of God Himself, who promises that the Holy Spirit will convict of sin. So plant the seed and trust that God will faithfully cause it to grow.

Question 43

What is someone doesn't believe that "taking God's name in vain" is a sin?

The Greek word used for "blasphemy" is *blasphemia*. *Blas* means "speech," and *phemia* means "against God or

50

sacred persons or things." Any speech against God is blasphemy. The apostle Paul considered himself a blasphemer before his conversion (1 Timothy 1:13) because he spoke against Jesus of Nazareth. But God's name is so holy that even using His name without due respect is considered blasphemy. People often use it casually and without meaning, as "just an expression," which God clearly condemns. How much more evil then is it to use His name as a cuss word to express disgust?

Another argument that may come up is that the Seventh Commandment refers only to adultery, not fornication (sex before marriage). That's not true. First Timothy 1:8–10 makes it clear that the Law condemns not only fornicators but also homosexuals.

> "When anyone dies, I ask myself, 'Was I faithful?' Did I speak all the truth? And did I speak it from my very soul every time I preached?"
> —CHARLES SPURGEON

Finally, some people point out that the Ninth Commandment says, "You shall not *bear false witness*." They maintain that this refers solely to giving false witness *in a court of law*, and therefore doesn't include everyday lying. Another untruth. First Timothy 1:8–10 also says that the Law was made for liars. So, as much as the world would like to do away with the Law, or at least water it down, it's immutable. It's not going away, and it will be the unbending standard of judgment on the day when God judges the hearts of men and women (see Romans 2:12).

Question 44

What if someone says the only Commandment they have ever broken is the one about lying? Do you press for more by going back over the Commandments, or do you just go with that single once-in-a-lifetime sin?

Committing even one sin, one time, is enough to send him to Hell (see James 2:10). But we know that every person has a multitude of sins. For starters, he has failed to love God with all of his heart, soul, mind, and strength. He has dishonored his parents' good name by being a liar. Besides that, you can't trust anything he says, because he is a self-admitted liar. However, I usually say, "There's bad news. *All* liars will have their part in the lake of fire" (Revelation 21:8). I explain that lying is very serious to God. The Bible says that "lying lips are an abomination to the Lord."

Question 45

What do you do when you've gone through the Law with someone, explained how Jesus paid his fine, and he was still unimpressed? The person's attitude seemed to be, *So what?* He just didn't grasp the gravity.

Remember that God resists the proud and gives grace to the humble (James 4:6), so don't feel compelled to give the Good News to a proud, self-righteous sinner. Only if he has been humbled by the Law is he ready for grace. Perhaps you didn't open up the Law and stir the conscience enough. So, soberly go through the Commandments again, and warn the person again, and then leave it in the hands of God. Pray that He brings conviction of sin.

Also keep in mind that different personalities react differently. Some people don't like to show their feelings. Others are a little dense. You can tell them that the plate is hot, but they remain unconvinced until they touch it. So don't go by your feelings. If you plant a garden, have confidence in the seed, water it as regularly as you can, then trust God to make the seeds grow.

Question 46

What if someone says that if God is good, then He must be all-forgiving? Someone asked me, "If God is all-forgiving and merciful, why do I need to do anything about my so-called sin? He'll forgive everyone no matter what, so why worry about a Hell?"

God is not "all-forgiving." He is just and holy. He will by no means clear the guilty (see Numbers 14:18), and any who are found guilty on Judgment Day will come under His terrible wrath. The "all-forgiving" god is an idol, so use the Law to reveal the holiness of God to your hearers.

Question 47

How do you respond to someone who says he doesn't care if he's going to Hell?

He doesn't believe that he's really going there. No one in his right mind would want to go to Hell, so you have to do your best to show him that there is such a place, and that God is right and just to send him there.

I often ask those who say they don't care if they've ever been in a dentist chair and had the drill hit a raw nerve. Most have. I then ask if they enjoyed the experience. Most didn't. Then I talk about what the Bible says Hell is like, and take them through the Law to show that they are heading there.

If you have been through the Law and they are still unconcerned, ask if they would sell an eye for a million dollars. Most won't. They value their eyes; they are above price. So how much more should they value the soul that looks out of those eyes? Don't be afraid to plead with the person.

Question 48

If you have walked through the "WDJD" outline of biblical evangelism and the person is not humble, but rather still in their pride and self-righteousness, do you stop there or do you present grace (Christ crucified) so they have the full gospel to consider? I'm thinking of Jesus' admonition in Matthew 7:6, "Do not give what is holy to the dogs; nor cast your pearls before swine, lest they trample them under their feet, and turn and tear you in pieces."

If they are proud, self-righteous, and contentious, leave the Law on them.

Then pray that they will humble themselves and be receptive to the message of grace. This is what Jesus did with the rich young ruler. He loved him, but He let him go without hearing of the love of God. Perhaps you could offer the person a tract and ask him to read it later.

Question 49

What if some people don't feel guilty over their sins (like having two wives, etc.) because of their culture?

There's no need to even go near an issue like polygamy. Instead, use the Law to produce enough guilt for him to see his need of God's mercy. When he sees that he's a liar, a thief, adulterer, etc., and trusts in the Savior, God Himself will, in time, convict him of any other cultural sins.

Question 50

What does it mean to have a seared conscience? Does it mean that the person is unreachable?

A "seared" conscience doesn't necessarily mean a *dead* conscience. Rather, it is one that is deadened on the outside. Sin sears the conscience until its muffled voice is no longer heard. This is a tragedy because the conscience in the voice of warning. Those who delight in sin, because they have dulled their conscience, are like a man who removes the batteries from his smoke detector because he doesn't want to be bothered by its alarm.

To awaken a deadened conscience, simply take the person through the Law. Address the conscience directly by saying, "You *know* it's wrong to lie, steal, commit adultery, etc." As you do so, the conscience will confirm the truth of the Commandments.

Question 51

How should I respond to someone who says, "Your religion is all about faith"?

Most of life is about faith. We put our faith in pilots when we trust them with our lives. Marriage is built on faith. So are business partnerships. So is friendship. I can't be mutual friends with someone I don't trust. We exercise faith when we eat food prepared by another person; we trust our weight to a chair when we sit in it. We have faith in history books, weather forecasters, politicians (well, maybe not). We place our faith in these items and people based on what we believe is evidence that they're trustworthy.

However, the questioner's statement implies that Christians are living by a naïve, blind faith based on something we can't see, when the opposite is the case. Our faith is rational and reasonable, based on credible, verifiable, historical evidence. The God who created us has given us all the evidence we need to come to know Him. You may want to recommend that atheists read the book *How to Know God Exists*. It's also important to explain the difference between believing something (the Bible), and trusting Someone (Jesus Christ).

Question 52

How can I prove that my Christian faith is "better" than other religions on a college campus?

All religions are manmade and are rooted in self-righteousness. Their followers are ignorant of God's righteousness (which comes via the Law), and because of that ignorance, they go about to establish their own righteousness. Only in Christianity is the believer given the righteousness of God through faith in Jesus Christ.

For more details, you may want to read our popular booklet called *Why Christianity?* It shows how the Christian faith is head and shoulders (understatement) above every other religion, and it does so without being condescending. It makes the reason for the cross make sense. According to one reviewer, "It is the best explanation of the gospel I've ever read." You can find them on our website (www.livingwaters.com) under "Booklets."

Question 53

How would you respond if someone asks, "How do you know that your belief in Christianity is right?"

If someone sincerely asks this question, then confine them under the Law and show them that it isn't a question of being "right." It's rather a question of having no alternative to the dilemma created by the Law. When a sinner sees sin in its true light, no self-righteous religion is going to satisfy the wrath of God against sin. The only salvation from death and Hell is the one that God provided in Jesus Christ. The Law throws a man into a burning desert. He is about to die of thirst when he looks up and sees that God is offering him a glass of cool, clear water in the gospel. There is no alternative to the grace of God in Christ.

Question 54

Some people argue that I believe Christianity only because I was raised in a Christian culture. When someone says, "If you had grown up in a different country or culture, you would believe in their religion," how should I respond?

This sounds complex, but it is quite simple. It is true that children do tend to adopt the religion they learned about from their parents. In all other religions, one automatically becomes a follower by birth, by being baptized as an infant, or by observing certain religious practices. But one becomes a Christian only by truly repenting of his sins and placing his trust in Jesus Christ alone for his salvation. It is entirely a work of God, and God will save whom He will no matter where they are located. God knows those whose hearts are truly seeking Him, and He ensures that they hear the gospel. He can reveal Himself to people even in the midst of Hindu, Muslim, or animist cultures, so they can put their trust in the Savior.

Always remember that believing something doesn't necessarily make it true. Only Christianity is backed up by objective, historical, archaeological, and experiential evidence to verify that it is true.

Question 55

How do I witness to someone who insists that God does not love her and who has decided to give her life to Satan?

She already belongs to Satan. Tell her that. He's her god.

He has blinded her mind. He's the spirit that works in the children of disobedience. He came to steal, kill, and destroy, and he is her father.

Don't tell her that God loves her. Keep the good wine until last. Tell her that God is angry at her because of her sin, and that's something she won't understand until you apply the Law to her conscience. If you leave the Law out of the equation, she will have a victim mentality, when she should see herself as a criminal.

Question 56

Where does the love of God come in when you're dealing with those who have the wrath of God upon them?

Pay attention to what the person you're witnessing to is saying. The mouth speaks out of the abundance of the heart. Is the person humble? Is he contrite? Is he sober in attitude? Or is he proud, self-righteous, trying to justify himself, etc.? The general rule is "Law to the proud, grace to the humble." You will have to make that call yourself as to when to bring in the cross. Only once people understand that they justly deserve God's wrath will His love displayed on the cross make sense.

> "They will never accept grace till they tremble before a just and holy Law. Therefore the Law serves a most necessary purpose, and it must not be removed from its place."
> —CHARLES SPURGEON

Question 57

How do you answer someone who says, "If God loves me so much, why are you telling me that and He isn't? Why do I have to read about it? How come God doesn't tell me Himself with His own voice?"

First, I would never speak of the love of God until I had opened up the Law and showed our sinful condition. The love of God isn't fully understood until the cross is understood. And the cross won't make much sense until there is a knowledge of sin. The more heinous the crime, the greater the mercy of the judge to acquit the criminal. The Law is what magnifies the love of God.

Besides, God did speak to Israel once and it was so terrifying they thought they were going to die. When God spoke to Jesus once, the Scriptures say that the people thought that it thundered. The fact is that God has chosen the foolishness of preaching to save those who believe. If the person wants God to speak further to him personally, he will have to read the Bible. We speak to God in prayer, and He speaks to us through His Word, and His Word tells us that He proved His love for us through the cross.

Question 58

I have a friend who is an atheist. I asked what kept her from believing in God and she said that she can't imagine one Being who cares about all the problems and wishes of everyone on earth. She said it's not logical. How can I explain to her about God's love for us in a way that she would understand?

Her concept of God is erroneous. He is not some sort of divine butler who is here to care for "all our problems and wishes." That may have been the picture painted for her by modern preachers, and so the god she can't believe in is an idol. It's no wonder she has no faith in it. It doesn't exist.

The way to show her God's love and His incredible, omnipotent power is to take her through the Commandments. Show her that she is a desperate criminal in the sight of a holy God, in danger of eternal damnation in a terrible place called Hell. That will help her to see that God is not a cosmic Santa Claus whose power is limited, but a just judge who is willing to save her if she will repent. Don't be concerned if she maintains that she doesn't believe in God. Tell her that she has to face Him anyway. Once she is born again and understands a little of God's absolute magnificence, then she will have no trouble believing that He can do anything.

Question 59

When I ask someone if he is saved and he sarcastically says, "Saved from what?" what is the proper response?

He almost has a right to be sarcastic (what Shakespeare called "the lowest form of wit"). As Christians, we should be careful when we use words like "saved," because they make no sense to an unbeliever. We put up signs that say things like "Jesus saves," and wonder why the world asks which bank He saves at. I would never ask a person if he is saved. I find that the best way to witness is to first begin in the natural realm, then ask what they think happens after someone dies—"What's on the other side?"

61

Question 60

In the Philippines, our culture (Filipino and Chinese) emphasizes respect for the elders. How can we go through the Ten Commandments, or even ask, "Would you consider yourself to be a good person?" or talk about death and Hell without sounding disrespectful? Older Chinese dislike hearing about death, so how could I share the gospel with them?

I think almost all of us feel very uncomfortable witnessing to elderly people we love and respect. But that's the point—if we love and respect them, we will talk to them. The reason they don't like talking about death is that they are afraid of dying (see Hebrews 2:14,15)—something that's true for all of us. You have found the answer for them, and if you care about them you will take courage and speak to them. The fear dissipates once you begin the conversation.

Just ask, "What do you think happens after someone dies?" That will let you know if you have a green or red light. If you are afraid that it will look as though you are pointing a finger, use your testimony when you share the gospel—e.g., "I didn't realize that lying lips were an abomination to the Lord and that all liars will end up in the lake of fire," etc.

Question 61

When someone says, "Well, I'm not perfect," or "No one is perfect," how do you respond biblically in light of Matthew 5:48?

Agree with the person. What he is seeking to do is justify his sinful heart, by spreading the blame around all of humanity and at the same time inferring that the standard God requires is too high. Play his game. Say, "That's right; you are not perfect. You are a self-admitted liar, thief, etc., and you have to stand before a perfect God whose Law you have violated and give an account of your actions. What are you going to say? You can't justify yourself. And you are right about no one being perfect. We have all sinned, and we are all heading for Hell."

The person's words reveal a subtle form of self-righteousness, and you have to chop that out with the sharp axe of the Law. So cut deep and get it all out. You want to bring him to a point of saying, "I have sinned against God." His sin is personal. Study Paul's use of the Law in Romans 2:21–23. He stirred the conscience and he made it personal. Nathan did the same thing with David when he said, "You are the man!" Study the opening verses of Psalm 51 to see how personal David knew his transgression was—knowledge that came from the prophet's rebuke. Count David's references to himself and his personal guilt (shown below in bold). Also notice that he calls what he did "evil" not just being "imperfect":

"Have mercy upon **me**, O God, according to Your lovingkindness; according to the multitude of Your tender mercies, blot out **my** transgressions. Wash **me** thoroughly from **my** iniquity, and cleanse **me** from **my** sin. For **I** acknowledge **my** transgressions, and **my** sin is always before **me**. Against You, You only, have **I** sinned, and done this evil in Your sight —that You may be found just when You speak, and blameless when You judge." (Psalm 51:1–4)

Question 62

I'm sometimes asked, "What about the people who have never heard of Jesus Christ—are you saying that they are all going to Hell?" That's been a very frequent and difficult one for me. How would you respond?

The inference is that the people who have never heard the gospel are basically good people, and that God would be unjust to send them to Hell. So, tell the questioner that they will be fine—if they are good people. However, in God's eyes a good person is one who is morally perfect in thought, word, and deed. That means that they will be in trouble with God if they have committed murder (hated), adultery (lust), theft, or if they have lied. God will do what is right and just, and will punish wrongdoing no matter where it's found. If they have broken even one Law, they will get what's coming to them. (This is dealt with in the first three chapters of the Book of Romans.) That's why we send missionaries to these people—so that they can be saved from their sins through faith in Jesus. Then say, "Now, let's get back to you . . ."

WITNESSING TO CERTAIN GROUPS

(How)

"What can be wiser than in the highest sense to bless our fellow men—to snatch a soul from the gulf that yawns, to lift it up to the Heaven that glorifies, to deliver an immortal from the thralldom of Satan, and to bring him into the liberty of Christ."
—CHARLES SPURGEON

Question 63

If management tells us not to witness at work anymore, are we supposed to stop sharing our faith? How can we reach our coworkers with the gospel?

If your boss forbids it, don't do it on work time. Instead, keep a pile of Million Dollar Bills or some other tract on your desk but don't give them out. If someone asks for one, let them take it. Show your faith by your works—let love shine. Give your coworkers small gifts (but not for the opposite sex—unless it's a gift from you and your spouse, with a card that says so).

I would also invite unsaved coworkers out to lunch (again, not the opposite sex), and witness to them there. Just ask for their thoughts on what happens after death. That will let you know if they are open to the gospel. If you detect contention, apologize and instead use closet prayer. Management can't stop you from praying, so determine that the more they stop you from witnessing, the more you are going to pray. Make a list of workers and uphold them before God, asking for divine openings.

Question 64

I became a believer about five months ago, and have been absolutely on fire for Christ ever since. My family is having a hard time dealing with that, just as I am having a hard time dealing with the fact that they are not saved. I have tried to witness to them, and show them through my actions the effect that Christ has had on my life, but they are becoming tired of listening. How can I effectively witness to my family members?

I know the frustration of having witnessed to friends and family, and they are still unconcerned about their salvation. You can't preach to them every time you see them; that would kill the relationship. It drives me crazy, though, that they could be snatched into Hell forever, and they don't really care.

Deal with your concerns for them in the prayer closet. Pray for them and then love them, not with words, but with actions. Instead of preaching, continue to show them your faith by your works. Buy gifts when it's not Christmas or a birthday. Mow lawns, wash dishes, clean cars. Be rich in good works so that they can see that your faith is genuine. Put yourself in their position. As far as they are concerned you have joined some religious cult. Prove them wrong by being sincerely loving, kind, and very down-to-earth. Then witness to them only if they bring the subject up. But make sure you pray for the opportunity and be watchful for it. In the meantime, witness to other Christians' unsaved loved ones, and trust that God will have some faithful Christian witness to yours.

Question 65

My mother is very hardened toward the gospel, and rarely lets me get a word in edge-wise when it comes to religion or politics. She appears to think that most Christians—with the exception of her best friend—are hypocrites, including me. What is the best way to witness to her?

Pray that her best friend witnesses to her. People often feel very uncomfortable speaking about spiritual things with a relative, but they will open up to a friend or stranger.

Why would your own mother think that you are a hypocrite? Make sure your life is without hypocrisy. Ask her what has caused her to think like that, and apologize if necessary. Then strive to honor and love her unconditionally.

Question 66

I am trying to share my faith with my father, who I only communicate with through email, and every time I try he either doesn't respond or gets angry. Can you give me any advice on how to make him understand when I can't talk to him face to face or have an actual conversation with him?

Make sure you are using the Law before grace. If he won't listen to you, you have other means of helping him. Pray for him, and openly show that you love him. Do anything you can to build a relationship with him. If someone sends you a humorous email, forward it to him. Send him gifts out of the blue. When you pray, believe that God will save him. That means no doubts, no fears, no worries. It means thanking God for His kindness in drawing your dad to Himself. Don't get caught up on issues of election; leave that up to God.

You may also want to check out the online evangelistic tools on our website (www.livingwaters.com), under "Free Evangelism Resources."

Question 67

I have a born-again daughter who has converted to Catholicism (her boyfriend is Catholic). I love her no matter what, but what can I say? Should I bring up the Ten Commandments?

I know this is painful to hear, but I wouldn't be too quick to say that your daughter is born again. If Jesus Christ is her Lord and Savior, she will not only love the truth, she will never be unequally yoked with an unbeliever. Roman Catholicism rests on a foundation of works as a means of salvation. It denies that we are saved by grace alone through faith alone, apart from works. If works are involved, then salvation isn't the gift of God (see Ephesians 2:8,9).

Only the self-righteous trust in works, so what you must do is chop down the roots of that poisonous tree. The only biblical and therefore effective means of doing that is to go through the Commandments. Put your daughter on the witness stand. Show her that she is a guilty criminal and that her good works are an attempt to bribe the Judge of the Universe. Use the Law as a schoolmaster to bring her to Christ. Drive her to the cross. When she repents and trusts in Jesus alone for her salvation, the Holy Spirit will then lead her into all truth. In the meantime, continue to pray for and love her as much as you can.

Question 68

What's the best way to witness to the elderly?

Elderly people who haven't come to faith are usually steeped in self-righteousness, and it is awkward for younger people to challenge them because of their age. It may therefore be easier to witness in the first person.

Instead of asking, "Have you ever lusted after someone?" you can say, "I didn't realize that God considered hatred the same as murder," etc.

Question 69

At what age can you begin to talk to children about salvation? I've gone through the process a number of times with my four children, ages six and under, but I also know that abstract reasoning will not begin until the age of nine or ten. So should wait to talk to our children until they're a certain age?

That depends upon their maturity. Some children come to Christ at a very young age, but it doesn't happen too often. The biblical thing to do is to train up the child in the way he should go. Teach him the Law. Soak him in Scripture. Teach him the fear of the Lord. We have a practical book called *How to Bring Your Children to Christ ... & Keep Them There*, which you may find very beneficial. It will help you avoid the heartbreaking trap of a false conversion in a child.

Question 70

How do I reach someone who is an adamant atheist without scaring him away? I have been trying to talk to this person every

> "Even with the light of nature, and the light of conscience, and the light of tradition, there are some things we should never have believed to be sins had we not been taught so by the Law."
> —CHARLES SPURGEON

chance I get about Jesus and the wonderful things He can do for us, but I don't seem to be getting anywhere. What can I do?

Listen to "Hell's Best Kept Secret" freely on our website to see how unbiblical it is to approach a proud person (which an atheist is) and talk about Jesus and the wonderful things He can do for them. We also have a TV episode called "God Has a Wonderful Plan" that addresses this subject. You can view it freely online at www.livingwaters.com (both of these can be found under "Free evangelism resources"). Your friend needs the Law. He needs to fear God. These teachings will help you know how to speak to him.

Question 71

How do you witness to people who believe in evolution and don't want to hear about God?

If you are unable to reason with them, there is little else you can do but pray for people who are close-minded. However, if their faith in evolution is strong enough to withstand a challenge—and they are open to considering whether the evidence supports their belief—you could give them the book *Evolution: A Fairytale for Grownups* or *How to Know God Exists: Scientific Proof of God*. The evidence presented in these books will give them compelling reasons to doubt their faith in the theory.

Question 72

How do you witness to a gnostic—someone who believes

that God is really evil, the serpent in Eden was really the Holy Spirit, and the knowledge that Jesus taught is what saves a person?

Don't address the character of God at this point. Instead, address the sin of this person by taking him through the Ten Commandments. Show him that he is a wicked criminal and that he has added to his sins by saying that God is evil. Lay it on thick and heavy. This is a terrible sin because it goes against the light of our conscience. We inherently know that God is good by nature, and to say that He is evil is odious.

Question 73

What do you say to people who believe in reincarnation?

Don't get sidetracked into discussing it. I normally ask what they think they will come back as and what they would like to be in the next life. I may ask what they did to merit coming back in this life as a human being, and who is in charge of dealing out all the new bodies . . . is it God? But I do it in a lighthearted way. Then I say, "If there is a place called Heaven, do you think that you are good enough to go there?" Then I take them through the Law. During that time I often mention that the Bible says "it is appointed for men to die once, but after this the judgment" (Hebrews 9:27).

Question 74

I presented the Law to a Muslim and he agreed God had a moral Law and admitted he would be found guilty.

However, he said that in Islam you will be punished "for a while" and then sent to Paradise. I kept asking how his fine is paid in the Muslim faith and he went back to punishment and then release to Paradise. I pointed out from Scripture that Hell is forever, not a temporary place of punishment. How would you have responded to this Muslim?

I would take him to civil court and give an example of a criminal who had raped and murdered a number of young girls. Paint the crime as being extremely heinous, because that's what sin is in God's sight. It is obvious that he doesn't see sin as being very serious, if it necessitates only temporal punishment. We tend to trivialize crimes against God with words like "fibs" and "white" lies, but the Scriptures tell us that "lying lips are an abomination to the LORD" (Proverbs 12:22). Lying is so serious in God's sight that all liars will have their part in the lake of fire. All you can do is plant the seed of truth and then pray that God makes your words (His truth) come to life in the man's heart.

Question 75

I have a Chinese coworker with whom I've shared the

gospel. I noticed some "decorations" hanging in his car, which he said were for "protection." Do I need to convince him to get rid of those things, or should I wait until he comes to Christ? I don't know if they have any spiritual power that could be in the way of his salvation, but how can I convince him that they are bad? I had a similar experience with a waitress who was wearing an ankh. She laughed when I told her it was dangerous to wear it and said she'd been wearing it for fifteen years.

I would dig a little further and ask him about what they actually do. Does he think they have any spiritual power? Where does God fit in with all this? Try to talk him out of trusting in them because they more than likely have some sort of negative spiritual power, although I don't believe they can stop him from coming to Christ (which is probably your concern). The Gadarene demoniac was full of demons, but he was still able to fall at the Savior's feet (see Luke chapter 8). You might want to get a copy of the book *Out of the Comfort Zone*. Chapter 10, "Invisible Realms," could open his eyes. It is frightening.

Question 76

How do you witness to someone who "accepted Christ" as a child but hasn't attended church as an adult and doesn't think he needs to?

The person has almost certainly had a false conversion, so you need to speak with him the same way you would speak to any other unsaved person. Don't feel intimidated by the fact that he has made a profession of faith. If it was genuine, he would be obedient to the Word of God.

I wouldn't even address the experience. Simply ask for his thoughts on the afterlife and ask whether he thinks he's good enough to go to Heaven. If he does, take him through the Law. If he speaks of salvation by grace, and that's what he is trusting in, ask him when he last read his Bible. If he is into the Word daily, tell him that it's important that he gets into fellowship, and then pray that he does. You can't do much more than that.

Question 77

When you ask strangers whether they are Christians and they say they are, but you suspect they may be false converts, how can you arrive at the truth concerning their salvation?

Most people in the United States think that they are "Christian." They think a Christian is someone who believes in God, or who isn't of another religious persuasion. So, ask if they have been "born again." If there is the slightest hesitation, be suspicious. Since some people believe they've been "born again" many times, you may want to say something like this (in a very friendly tone): "I love to hear how people come to know the Lord. Would you mind sharing your personal testimony?"

Two other probing questions are, "Do you consider yourself to be a good person?" (false converts usually do), and "When did you last read your Bible?"

Question 78

What do you say to a "Christian" who has a beer in one hand and a cigarette in the other?

I would ask him when he last read his Bible; does he think that he's a good person, etc. If he is reading the Word daily and seems to have a good understanding of salvation, I would gently let him know that he should pray about how he presents himself. He should be without reproach, and not even eat meat if it offends a brother. Tell him that what he is doing is offensive to you and it may be a stumbling block to others. He is also defiling the temple of the Holy Spirit by abusing it with known poisons.

Question 79

How would you witness to someone who has grown up in church, knows who God is and what Christianity means, but says that he has too much fun sinning and will just accept Christ later so he can go to Heaven when he dies?

This person lacks a fear of God. As always, this traces itself back to idolatry. As a child he was probably taught that Jesus is your buddy and the celestial problem-solver, and then in church heard the message of the modern gospel. He needs to have the fear of God put into him. Take him through the Law, speak of future punishment, and point out that God may kill him before he makes his decision to "accept" Christ. Put him on the witness stand; show him that he is a devious criminal who is about to be executed and sent to an everlasting and fearful Hell.

Do it in love and in gentleness, but reprove and rebuke him, with all longsuffering and doctrine. Tell him what Jesus said in Matthew 7:21–23, and remind him about how God called a man a fool because he put off his salvation, and trusted that he had many days ahead of him (see Luke 12).

Question 80

What do you do when a Christian friend is falling out of the will of God? He knows the Ten Commandments, but doesn't see anything wrong with what he is doing and gets angry when I try to talk to him about it.

I assume you are saying that he is willfully getting into sin. This is a sign of a false conversion. I would send a loving letter, saying that you are deeply concerned for him. I would suggest that you first read 1 John chapters 1–3 and Matthew chapter 7.

Question 81

How do you witness to someone you know well who is devoutly religious, yet you still question their salvation? How do you avoid sounding as if you are judging them? I have several friends who are very religious, but I think they are trying to earn their salvation by doing good works.

I know that this can be uncomfortable. However, think about how you would feel if this friend was killed in a car accident tonight. If you care about that person you must say something. So many people that we know now as on-fire, God-loving, evangelizing Christians were once in the category of either being religious or a false convert, and they are eternally grateful that someone brought them the true gospel.

The "religious" are those who are trusting in their own efforts to obtain salvation, and there are millions in this category. But the false converts are those who are just as deceived. They are those who name the name of Christ, profess a new-birth experience, but don't have the things that accompany salvation. There is no evidence that they are truly saved. There are millions of false converts also. These categories of people need to be awakened (with God's help), by those who care enough to risk offending them.

Both religious people and false converts can usually be traced back to idolatry. These people don't have an understanding of God's nature. They therefore lack the fear of God and of the truth of salvation by grace alone though faith alone. They are self-righteous. So how do you handle this?

> "The preacher's work is to throw sinners down in utter helplessness, so that they may be compelled to look up to Him who alone can help them."
> —CHARLES SPURGEON

Simply say, "Dave, can I ask you an important question? Do you consider yourself to be a good person?" That will reveal whether he is trusting in his own righteousness or in the cross. It will show you if he understands the gravity of sin. If he says that he is a good person, take him through the Commandments. If he admits his sins, but says that he is trusting in Jesus for his salvation, say, "But, Dave, you told me that you think that you are a good person, when Jesus said there is none good but God" (see Mark 10:18).

Ask him if he is reading his Bible *every* day. The odds are that he won't be. It may be every second or third day, or once a week, or never. Ask him how he would rate his walk with the Lord, on a scale of one to ten. Tell him that it should be ten for every one of us. We are to love the Lord our God with all of our heart, soul, mind, and strength.

Then point out that Jesus said many will say to Him, "Lord, Lord," on the Day of Judgment, and He will say, "I never knew you; depart from Me, you who practice lawlessness!"(Matthew 7:21–23). Talk to him about the reality of false conversion and the importance of manifesting the fruit of repentance. Tell him that there is nothing more important than his eternal salvation. Then you could perhaps pray with him, encouraging him to make his calling and election sure. The very fact that you have taken him through the Law will bring a sense of sobriety to him about sin (if he is honest of heart). Then keep him in prayer. Of course, it goes without saying that you use a very loving and concerned tone as you speak with him.

Another approach would be to tell him, "I just listened to an alarming message about the reality of false conversion. Have you ever thought about that—how you can know whether you're truly saved?" Then give him a copy of the message "True and False Conversion" on CD.

Question 82

How do I share the Law with someone whom I have already shared the modern gospel with?

If the person is still open to listening, you could earnestly say, "I realize our previous conversations may not have made much sense. Can I share something that will help it be more understandable?"

Question 83

How do you witness to Mormons?

It is very easy to become caught up in arguing about the error of Mormonism. Mormons are ready to defend their religion; they know how to defuse and divert the average Christian's arguments. The key to reaching them is to uncover what they are trusting in for their salvation. They believe that grace isn't enough to save them, so they have to add to the grace of God to be saved. Calvary wasn't enough. This error comes from a wrong concept of God's nature, and therefore a wrong concept of sin. So try saying this to any of the cults: "I have a knife in my back and three minutes to live. My life is draining from my body. What do I have to do to enter the Kingdom of God?"

Those in cults will usually tell you that you will have to do something to be saved, revealing that the salvation they offer is works based. From there, simply ask the person if he thinks that he is a good person. If he does, take him through the Law and show him that he has sinned against God and that the only thing that can save him is God's mercy. The right use of the Law will put *earned* salvation so far from him that mercy can be his only option. Any works on his part are an attempt to bribe the Judge of the Universe, and God will not be bribed on Judgment Day.

For more details, we have episodes on how to reach Jehovah's Witnesses and Mormons in the Third Season of "The Way of the Master." You may like to watch those.

Question 84

How do you witness to those who are grieving over the death of a loved one? Do you use the Law in the same way as you would with anyone? As a pastor I preach at funerals for the unsaved on a regular basis. While I never comment on the eternal destiny of the deceased, I always preach the gospel plainly and use the Law. Is it advisable to do this?

It is advisable to share the gospel whenever and wherever we can. You are wise not to comment on any person's eternal destiny. We are usually not privy to conversations sinners have with the Lord in the last moments of life. I say "usually" because we were allowed to hear what was whispered between one repentant thief on a cross and Jesus. God only knows how many sinners say, "Lord, remember me . . . ," and Jesus hears them.

When the unsaved lose a loved one they are often open, perhaps for the first time in their lives, to the questions of eternity. So preach to them as though it was your last sermon, and as though it was your audience's last day on earth.

Question 85

How do you respond to a devout Catholic whose brother died unsaved? An old high school friend called me about the death of his brother, a devout Catholic who was killed in a motorcycle accident while drunk. My friend believes in praying to saints, Mary (being the mother of all), praying the rosary, purgatory, etc. I didn't want to hurt him by saying that people who don't place Jesus first in their lives and who pray to saints and Mary are lost. When he asked me to pray for his brother's soul in purgatory, I said that I couldn't pray for his brother but I could pray for him. He became angry and said his brother was trapped in purgatory and needed our prayers to get him out. I told him that wasn't biblical at all and that our souls go to either Heaven or Hell (no purgatory). As I explained that Jesus died for us so we wouldn't have to go to Hell and started witnessing with the Law and grace, he ended the conversation and I never heard from him again.

I admire your love and courage. You did the right thing, so don't be discouraged. Make sure you attempt to stay in contact with your friend. I once had to do something similar with my Catholic aunt (not quite as dramatic as your situation). She said that she had been praying to her dead husband. I told her that he wasn't omniscient and that she should never speak to the dead. It was very awkward for me, but I had to tell her the truth even though it might be offensive to her. The next day she gave me a check for $1,000, out of the blue. I was very surprised, but delighted, because we had just pulled our three kids out of secular school and were putting them into a Christian school, and the money covered the costs. You didn't get a check from an aunt, but I am sure you have your Father's smile.

Question 86

I've found that many of the homeless in our city have been greatly affected by drugs and other things, causing their minds to be permanently damaged. How do I get through to people like this and those with slight metal illnesses?

Keep the gospel very simple. Patiently explain it until the person understands the issues, and then have confidence in God and in the power of the gospel. Obviously, pray with and for the person. Always remember this great truth: With God, nothing shall be impossible. There are plenty of Christians who can testify that it was only upon conversion that God gave them a sound mind.

Question 87

Is there ever a time when you think someone isn't worth approaching because they are inappropriately attired or are very drunk? Although we care and don't want anyone to go to Hell, we also don't want to get ourselves into a bad situation.

I have found that the people with the meanest looking

tattoos and hooks through their nose are often the friendliest. Few others approach them because they look scary, so when someone does it surprises them. When I see people wearing filthy T-shirts with disgusting words on them, my initial reaction is to despise them. Instead I approach them and I am almost always delighted by what I find. Try it.

Regarding drunks, it really depends on how drunk they are. You have to take each case on its own merit. Some drunks get angry, so you are wise to be careful with them.

Question 88

How do you deal with demon-possessed people when you are witnessing to them?

Demonic possession may be much more prevalent than most of us assume. The Bible tells us, "And you He made alive, who were dead in trespasses and sins, in which you once walked according to the course of this world, *according to the prince of the power of the air, the spirit who now works in the sons of disobedience*, among whom also we all once conducted ourselves in the lusts of our flesh, fulfilling the desires of the flesh and of the mind, and were by nature children of wrath, just as the others" (Ephesians 2:1–3, emphasis added). There is a spirit that works in the unsaved, and now and then it is obvious that someone is demonically possessed. The way to deal with them is to do so very gently. Ask the person for his name. Jesus did this. If the individual is spilling over with demons, he (they) may give you a strange demonic name. If he gives you what sounds like his real name, use it as you speak to him. People are less likely to attack you if you use their name when speaking to them. Also, keep in mind that demons cannot stop someone from coming to Christ. Look at Scripture:

> Then they came to the other side of the sea, to the country of the Gadarenes. And when He had come out of the boat, immediately there met Him out of the tombs a man with an unclean spirit, who had his dwelling among the tombs; and no one could bind him, not even with chains, because he had often been bound with shackles and chains. And the chains had been pulled apart by him, and the shackles broken in pieces; neither could anyone tame him. And always, night and day, he was in the mountains and in the tombs, crying out and cutting himself with stones.
>
> When he saw Jesus from afar, he ran and worshiped Him. And he cried out with a loud voice and said, "What have I to do with You, Jesus, Son of the Most High God? I implore You by God that You do not torment me."
>
> For He said to him, "Come out of the man, unclean spirit!" Then He asked him, "What is your name?"
>
> And he answered, saying, "My name is Legion; for we are many." (Mark 5:1–9)

Notice a number of things about this demon-possessed man. He was self-destructive, attracted by death and darkness, he was tormented, and he was supernaturally strong. But the demons didn't stop him from running to Jesus and worshiping Him. So realize that fact and take the person through the Law, very thoroughly.

He needs to shut to door to sin and not "give place to the devil" (Ephesians 4:27). The key for any person to be free from the demonic realm is to obey the command: "Submit to God. Resist the devil and he will flee from you" (James 4:7).

One other point. Don't chase after the demonic realm. It will more than likely chase after you. Paul was followed by a demon-possessed woman for many days, before he lost patience and dealt with her.

"My anxious desire is that, every time I preach, I may clear myself of the blood of all men; that if I step from this platform to my coffin, I may have told out all I knew of the way of salvation."
—CHARLES SPURGEON

OPEN-AIR
PREACHING

(How)

"The open-air speaker's calling is as honorable as it is arduous, as useful as it is laborious. God alone can sustain you in it, but with Him at your side you will have nothing to fear."
—CHARLES SPURGEON

Question 89

Since open-air preaching is mentioned numerous times in Scripture, why does it seem that Christians respond negatively to it, and I have never heard it preached on?

Unfortunately, there are a few weirdoes who scream at and abuse people as they walk by. These are the ones who make it onto the TV news or are depicted in movies. So you can't blame some people for having a negative attitude toward open-air preaching. However, that's a cross we have to carry.

We don't hear many pastors preaching on the subject, probably because they don't open-air preach. Let's hope and pray that that changes. Your example may help. When you stand up and break the sound barrier, never forget, you are in the best of company. Jesus, Paul, Stephen, Wesley, Whitefield, and Spurgeon were open-air preachers. There are no better steps to follow in.

Question 90

What advice would you give someone who has never done open-air preaching, but wants to start?

You are needed to "go into the world," so don't listen to your fears. You are going to get them (I still do). They will be so real that they'll make you sweat. But don't listen; just do it.

Have you ever felt the joy of sharing the gospel with someone who is genuinely listening to every word you are saying? Multiply that by 150. That's a good open-air session. There's nothing like it when you have a good heckler, and a crowd of people listening to the words of everlasting life.

Question 91

What is the difference between messages preached in the open air and those preached in a building where people are sitting and attentive?

People in a church building are there willingly and are a captive audience. In the open air, if they don't like what you are saying or you are boring, they leave. Therefore, you need to learn the *skills* of open-air preaching. The analogy of "fishing" for men is so applicable. A good fisherman is a skilled fisherman, and his skill comes by experience. He learns to go where the fish gather. He knows that seagulls gather where the fish are, or that certain seaweeds attract certain fish. He knows how to bait a hook so that it is disguised. He knows when to reel in the fish, etc. These skills come by experience, but for more in-depth teaching to hasten that experience you can watch our DVD called "Open-Air Preaching 4-in-1."

Question 92

What are your thoughts on women open-air preaching?

While there is controversy about a woman's role in the church, there is no question about the beneficial nature of having women involved in the task of evangelism. The first evangelists were women. They took the good news of the resurrection to the disciples, who were cringing behind locked doors. While there are a few who would raise an eyebrow at the thought of a woman preaching in the open air, it is biblical. Here's why. Can you think of any verse that forbids a woman from sharing the gospel with a Hell-bound sinner? Of course not. She is commissioned to share her faith. May she witness to two people at once? Of course. How about twenty people at once? How about in an open-air situation where she gets to share the everlasting gospel with one hundred sinners?

Question 93

What is a good way to practice open-air preaching before doing it "live"?

Go over the gospel in your mind until it's second nature —no, until it's first nature. When you are alone, preach it. (In the shower is a great place to preach.) Go through a few anecdotes. Get used to the sound of your own voice. Pretend to engage a heckler. Invite some friends over and practice what you preach.

Question 94

How do you evaluate a good place to station yourself?

Find a place where people gather—beaches, parks, or waiting in line—where they're not in a hurry. Select a place that has plenty of foot traffic, away from the noise of the street, a fountain, or machinery. It is ideal to have somewhere that will acoustically hold your voice, and where you can be slightly elevated. You shouldn't have problems speaking in public places in the United States; it is your First Amendment right to speak on American soil.

Question 95

How consistently do you stay in one area? Do you constantly try new places?

I will keep going back to an area as long as people will listen to the gospel. This is because it is good for regulars to hear the gospel more than once. You will find that you can befriend these people, and some may even seek you out with questions. Another reason I stick with the same place is because of the old adage, "If it's not broke, why fix it?" This is also true then you find an effective fishing hole for handing out tracts and witnessing.

Question 96

How do you deal with people that you see again in the same place you had previously open aired?

Try to remember their names and greet them when you see them. If they keep coming back, ask them questions. You may find that you have the blessing of a regular heckler.

Question 97

Do you go by yourself to preach? If not, how many Christians should go with you?

The more laborers there are, the better. A crowd tends to draw a crowd. Just make sure that your helpers don't argue with hecklers or distract your listeners while you're speaking. Tell them to pay attention and not become distracted and talk to each other. One of the most helpful things your team can do is clap when people answer trivia correctly. Nothing attracts people like applause and laughter. Instruct your helpers to follow those who peel away from the crowd, and either give them a tract or try to engage them in conversation.

> "If any man's life at home is unworthy, he should go several miles away before he stands up to preach. When he stands up, he should say nothing."
> —CHARLES SPURGEON

Question 98

How do you draw a crowd, if offering money as a prize doesn't work?

I have tried everything under the sun. Some things work and some don't. The best way I have found to generate interest is to engage someone in conversation. Don't wait until someone heckles you or asks you a question—you ask them. Call on people who stop and listen. Say, "You, sir! Do you think that there's a Heaven? Why/why not? Do you think that you are a good person?" Keep at it until his initial shock of being "picked on" wears off.

Some of the best hecklers I've had came from me prompting them. So be bold.

Question 99

Do you add any entertainment, such as someone playing a guitar and singing?

If singing would help me get a crowd, I would sing, if I could. I am serious. If I could sing, dance, or juggle, I would use that skill for the glory of God. If I could smash wood with my fist, I would use that skill to pull in a crowd. If you have a talent of any sort, give serious consideration to using it to reach the lost.

Question 100

Do you post gospel texts around where you preach?

The Bible tells us that sinners hate the light. So I don't even hold a Bible when I preach. I don't want people to have a prejudicial attitude toward the gospel.

Question 101

What is the most effective way to keep a crowd after revealing the Law?

There are two ways. One is to engage a colorful heckler. By that, I mean one who will speak up and then be quiet while you address his question. The other way is to make sure you preach with passion. People will often listen to you if you speak with conviction.

Question 102

Are contending for the faith and being a bit contentious to draw/maintain the crowd the same thing?

Of course, you want to always make sure you are respectful, congenial, and uncompromising. But people won't stay and listen to a boring preaching, so you have to be on the edge. It's difficult to try to explain. Christians sometimes think that it's unloving to speak in such a way, but it is most necessary if you want to hold your hearers. If you listened to me share the gospel with one or two people, you would probably notice an obvious gentleness in my tone. However, if you listen to me preach in the open air, it may seem contentious and provocative. This is because if I preached the same way I speak, I would never hold a crowd. It is important in both cases that I am motivated by love, but if I don't keep the preaching "on the edge," I will lose my hearers in minutes (if not seconds).

John Wesley put it this way: "In the streets a man must from beginning to end be intense, and for that very reason he must be condensed and concentrated in his thought and utterance." This "intense" preaching may be misunderstood by those who don't know why it's there. The problem is that when we read the Gospels, we don't see the passion involved in its discourses. When Jesus spoke, there were those in the crowd who hated Him and wanted to kill Him. People undoubtedly called out, accusing Him of blasphemy, etc., or asked Him questions. Without a doubt, the atmosphere would have been electric. That's the atmosphere that holds a crowd's attention. To become passive in the name of love and gentleness will pull the plug out and the electricity will immediately leave.

So be ready, because you may be accused of preaching without love. The accusations almost always come from those brethren who have never preached in the open air. When speaking of open-air preaching, R. A. Torrey said, "Don't be soft. One of these nice, namby-pamby, sentimental sort of fellows in an open-air meeting, the crowd cannot and will not stand. The temptation to throw a brick or a rotten apple at him is perfectly irresistible, and one can hardly blame the crowd."

Question 103

If police or security officers try to shut us down, how do we effectively deal with them so they'll enable us to continue?

Be very polite. Don't talk about First Amendment rights (that upsets them). Instead ask the officer or security guard if you are breaking the law. If you are, you will gladly leave. If you aren't breaking any law, gently tell them that you are going to keep speaking.

Question 104

How do you get a license to preach on a college campus?

Call the campus, tell them you'd like to come and speak, and ask for their requirements. They may let you speak with or without amplification. You may need some sort of insurance, or they may want to restrict you to a certain area. If there is a Christian organization on the campus that invites you, that usually gets around any red tape.

Question 105

Has there ever been a time doing open-air or even one-to-one when you just didn't know what to say? If you draw a blank while speaking or when someone asks you a question, how do you respond without looking like a complete idiot? It's never happened, but this is my fear.

Keep a New Testament with you and if you freeze up, say, "I would just like to read something to you." Read John 3:16–18 and conclude with, "Thank you for listening." *Just knowing that you have that option will dissipate the fear.*

If someone asks you a question that you don't know how to answer, simply say, "I'm sorry, I don't know the answer to that." There's nothing wrong with a humble admission. In fact, it may speak volumes more to your hearers than an eloquent answer.

Question 106

Are there certain Scriptures that are more effective or applicable in open-air preaching than in a one-to-one encounter?

They are the same Scriptures that you would use in one-to-one. Make sure they are verses that open up the Commandments, and that speak of the cross, repentance, and faith.

Question 107

If you don't sense a conviction of sin as you are preaching to a crowd, would you still give the grace part of the sermon?

When open-air preaching, I would. This is because I don't trust my senses. It may seem like a contentious crowd, but there could be one person in that crowd who is listening.

Question 108

What would you say is the most important thing to remember about preaching open-air?

We can easily get so caught up in apologetics that we forget to preach the cross. And it's easy to do because it is intellectually stimulating. It's important to always remember that apologetics address the intellect and don't bring conviction of sin. I have seen many open-air situations where the discussion goes on and on and degenerates into an argument. It is the cross that a sinner needs to hear about. Paul said, "For I determined not to know anything among you except Jesus Christ and Him crucified" (1 Corinthians 2:2). In Athens, Paul used apologetics (briefly) as a highway to the cross. That was his destination. Apologetics should be a means to an end, not the end itself. So always keep that in mind, both in preaching and in personal witnessing.

GENERAL
WITNESSING
QUESTIONS

(How)

"We want in the Church of Christ a band of well-trained sharpshooters, who will pick the people out individually and be always on the watch for all who come into the place, not annoying them, but making sure that they do not go away without having had a personal warning, invitation, and exhortation to come to Christ."
—CHARLES SPURGEON

Question 109

When Paul spoke in Athens, why did he begin his preaching with creation as opposed to the Law (Acts 17:24)?

In Acts 17:16 we are told that Paul was grieved because the whole city of Athens was given over to idolatry. So, in verses 22–28, he tells his hearers that they had other gods before the God of creation. He is in essence opening up the First and the Second of the Ten Commandments: "I am the LORD your God...You shall have no other gods before Me. You shall not make for yourself a carved image" (Exodus 20:2–4). Then, in verses 29–31, he rebukes them for their idolatry and preaches repentance and future punishment by the Law ("in righteousness"). So I wouldn't say that he began with creation *as opposed to* the Law. It was what he used to point them to the Law.

Think of how Jesus approached the woman at the well (in John 4). He began to speak to her about water, but then He spoke to her about her violation of the Seventh Commandment. When Nathan was commissioned by God to reprove David for his sins, Nathan began in the natural realm, and then pointed out David's transgression: "Why have you despised the commandment of the LORD?"

Although Paul mentioned creation, he didn't stay there for long, because speaking about creation doesn't convict a man of his sins. There is no guilty conscience accusing hearers as long as we speak apologetically. The goal is to use the Law to bring the knowledge of sin.

Many times I have been caught up in a sword fight about evolution or atheism, and I've suddenly realized that little progress was being made. These subjects should

103

merely be seen as a means to an end. The end is the preaching of the reality of Judgment Day and the terror of Hell—the cross, repentance, and faith—and the biblical way there is through the Law. You can see Paul do this as he exposes their idolatry (First and Second Commandments) and preaches future punishment for sin (see Acts 17:29–31).

Question 110

How often do you preach on a subject such as abortion, rather than the straightforward Good Person test? How does this work out in terms of audience participation, producing conviction, etc.?

We should speak about social sins (pornography, pedophilia, fornication, drunkenness, drug abuse, etc.), but always keep the Law hovering over the sinner. Otherwise, you will just be seen as a "holier-than-thou" preacher. The Law will keep focus on the fact that it is *God* who is offended by sin, and it is God to whom we are all answerable. We can bring up the wickedness of abortion when we open up the Sixth Commandment. However, it is a very emotional subject (and so it should be), so don't get into a shouting match with an angry person. Say that it's murder and the blood of the murdered child is on the hands of those who took its life, then move on. Remember, it is the Law that brings conviction of sin, so that's what we want to focus on

Question 111

Do you think it is best to have interaction, asking

questions, etc., with the audience, or straightforward preaching?

Whether you are talking to one person, two people or two hundred, it is wonderful to have people ask questions. Just make sure you stay in control of the direction of the conversation. Don't get sidetracked, and don't get into arguments.

Question 112

If you encounter people who are willing to talk, but have lots of questions about Christianity, other religions, etc., how much time do you spend with them versus moving on to someone else who might be more "ripe for harvest," if you will? I don't mean people who are antagonistic; I mean people who have genuine concerns or issues that they've been struggling with.

People who keep asking questions don't see the urgency of the issue. There comes a point where you have to ask, "If you died right now, where would you go?" If the person is unsaved, you want him to give the right answer: "Hell." Then ask, "What you are you going to do about it?" You want him to say that he will repent and trust the Savior. Then you ask, "When are you going to do that?" You want him to say, "Right now." If he hasn't come to that point, then you need to put the screws on.

Take the person through the Law again and show him that he is a criminal who has been commanded by God Himself to repent and trust in the Savior. The time has come to stop the questions for the moment and do what He commands. Then, once he is right with God, he can look into those questions, if he still has them.

Question 113

How do you deal with multiple objections from different people that come to you at almost the same time?

Whether you are preaching open-air or speaking to a small handful, you have to take control. Just say, "One at a time, please. Sir, please let the lady speak first," etc. Speak with authority or you will have a circus on your hands.

"Let eloquence be flung to the dogs rather than souls be lost. What we want is to win souls. They are not won by flowery speeches."

—CHARLES SPURGEON

Question 114

How do you respond to someone who heads off your witnessing effort by quoting "judge not, lest ye be judged"?

Jesus told His disciples not to judge *each other*. That command doesn't mean that we are not to make moral judgments. He also tells us that when we judge, we should use "righteous judgment" (John 7:24). And isn't the person who's accusing you of being judgmental making a judgment about you? It's important to make it clear that whenever we speak about sin we *are* making a moral judgment, but it is based on God's standards, not ours. The moral Law is the righteous standard by which all of

106

us will be judged. So, helping people see how they'll do when they stand before God on Judgment Day it isn't being judgmental—it's being compassionate.

Question 115

When someone refuses to complete the Good Person test, how do I end the conversation on a good note? For example, if they say, "I don't want to continue this conversation," how can I respond?

That is difficult. It doesn't happen very often, but when it does I say that I am sorry for offending them and that I hope they have a nice day. You never know what their experience may be. Perhaps they have had a friend who was pulled into a religious cult and they are paranoid of being deceived. Or maybe they have just lost a loved one and the pain is too much to take. The way you conclude the conversation may be a witness to them, so go out of your way to be kind, understanding, loving, and gentle.

Question 116

How important is it to know the verse references when witnessing?

It is important to know your way around the Bible, but with computers you can find a Scripture in seconds. So don't fear that someone is going to ask, "Where is that in the Bible?" It rarely happens, and you can always say, "I will find out for you and let you know." The odds are that they don't really care.

Question 117

What do you do when you're using the Law in a group situation and a Christian starts to diffuse the power of the Law by mentioning grace too soon?

I ask him to please wait and listen to what I am saying, and then share his thoughts in a few moments. That usually works.

Question 118

What do you do when other Christians tear down or take away the seed that has been planted?

I seriously struggle to keep my cool. They will listen to me open up the Law, speak of Judgment Day and Hell, and then say something like, "That doesn't sound very loving to me." When I hear that, I pray for special grace and turn my attention to them for a moment and question them in front of their friend or the crowd. It usually goes something like this: "Where will this man go if he dies in his sins?" The professing Christian usually says, "He will be separated from God." So I press him: "What is the name of the place where he will go to?" He will say, "To a terrible place."

I press him further as to what it's called. When I finally get him to say the word "Hell," I say, "That's not very loving . . . or is it? If you believe he would go to Hell for all eternity, do you warn him, or do you let him go there unwarned? If you care about this man, then let me talk to him about his salvation and you quietly pray that God helps me. Thanks." That approach usually works. I then approach him afterwards, shake his hand, and give him a CD of "Hell's Best Kept Secret."

Question 119

If you find yourself losing your patience, what do you do?

I remember once feeling very impatient with some hecklers. I could feel anger in my eyes, so I said to the crowd, "I'll be back in a few moments." I found somewhere quiet and asked God to forgive me for impatience. The break and the prayer did help.

Question 120

How do you redeem yourself when you have done something very wrong—sinned, became angry, misstated Scripture, let the crowd get out of hand, provoked a sinner to anger, gave a "watered down" presentation of the gospel, etc.?

You simply apologize where necessary. Ask God for forgiveness. Then learn from your mistakes. We all make them, so don't be discouraged. Don't allow them to become stumbling blocks, rather let them be stepping stones. Bruises give us memories to help us to avoid future pitfalls.

Question 121

How do you avoid things that will tempt you and may even cause you to stumble as you go into the darkness (lust, coveting)?

I currently open-air preach at Huntington Beach in Southern California, where people wear "string" as an excuse for a bathing suit. If you find yourself in these situations you have to let the fear of the Lord be your guide. Deal with it in prayer before you go, and if you stumble with your eyes, be very quick to repent. If it becomes a problem, avoid such places.

Question 122

What if you are confronted with a serious personal situation with a stranger that requires immediate help? What do you do if you don't know what to do?

It sounds like you are concerned about "giants" in the land. I have never had that happen. So cast down your imaginations, and if by chance something like this does happen, God will give you the wisdom you need to handle it.

ENDING THE ENCOUNTER

(How)

"God never clothes men until He has first stripped them, nor does He quicken them by the gospel till first they are slain by the Law. When you meet with persons in whom there is no trace of conviction of sin, you may be quite sure that they have not been wrought upon by the Holy Spirit; for 'when He is come, He will reprove the world of sin, and of righteousness, and of judgment.'"
—CHARLES SPURGEON

Question 123

I've noticed that sometimes after you witness to people you encourage them to pray a prayer of repentance and faith later. Is this because you discern that they aren't ready to truly give their life to Jesus right then? I see the wisdom in not rushing a person to make a decision (we don't want to make a false convert), but wouldn't it be good to have them pray right then (if they have acknowledged their sin and understand the gospel) as long as we don't follow that prayer by saying, "Congratulations, you're saved"? Shouldn't we have them pray before the conviction wears off? What if the actual verbalizing of a prayer makes something "click" in their heart? Isn't waiting potentially as dangerous as rushing the person?

Our methodology reveals our theology. If the conviction is there, it's only because the Holy Spirit is doing the convicting. That means that God's hand is on him, and he will come to Christ in God's timing. I don't ever want to interfere with a work of God. Another reason I ask if they would like to pray later (on TV) is that there is something very awkward about surrendering to Christ on camera. This is because I don't pray a "sinner's prayer" with him, but instead ask if he wants to pray a prayer of repentance, then I pray for him. Confessing and forsaking your sins is very personal, and I don't want to push someone into something they don't want to do. Remember, people aren't saved by verbalizing a prayer, but by their heartfelt repentance and surrender to Christ. God knows their heart.

Question 124

Doesn't your teaching state that one shouldn't lead someone in a "sinner's prayer"?

I *do* believe in praying with sinners who come to Christ. The following is from *The Evidence Bible* (commended by Franklin Graham and Dr. Kennedy):

To Pray or Not to Pray?

The question often arises about what a Christian should do if someone is repentant. Should we lead him in what's commonly called a "sinner's prayer" or simply instruct him to seek after God? Perhaps the answer comes by looking to the natural realm. As long as there are no complications when a child is born, all the doctor needs to do is *guide the head*. The same applies spiritually. When someone is "born of God," all we need to do is guide the head—make sure that they *understand* what they are doing. Philip the evangelist did this with the Ethiopian eunuch. He asked him, "Do you understand what you read?" (Acts 8:30). In the parable of the sower, the true convert (the "good soil" hearer) is he who hears "and understands." This understanding comes by the Law in the hand of the Spirit (Romans 7:7). If a sinner is ready for the Savior, it is because he has been drawn by the Holy Spirit (John 6:44). This is why we must be careful to allow the Holy Spirit to do His work and not rush in where angels fear to tread. Praying a "sinner's prayer" with someone who isn't genuinely repentant may leave you with a stillborn in your hands.

Therefore, rather than *lead* him in a prayer of repentance, it is wise to encourage him to pray himself. When

Nathan confronted David about his sin, he didn't lead the king in a prayer of repentance. If a man committed adultery, and his wife is willing to take him back, should you have to write out an apology for him to read to her? No. Sorrow for his betrayal of her trust should spill from his lips. She doesn't want eloquent words, but simply sorrow of heart. The same applies to a prayer of repentance. The words aren't as important as the presence of "godly sorrow." The sinner should be told to repent—to confess and forsake his sins. He could do this as a whispered prayer, then you could pray for him. If he's not sure what to say, perhaps David's prayer of repentance (Psalm 51) could be used as a model, but his own words are more desirable.

The following letter is typical: "I just want to let you know that about a year ago I was thinking about the people that I had led in the sinner's prayer. I couldn't think of one who was actually in church and growing in their faith. I began to look closer at the Word and ask the Lord to please show me if I was doing something wrong. Not much time passed until I came upon the WOTM website. I watched the videos, looked up the Scripture references, and it all made so much sense. I have Ray's 101 lessons and am working through the lessons. Thanks!" —D. Jones

Question 125

Are altar calls biblical? If they aren't, then why are so many evangelical churches doing them?

The altar is mentioned often in the Scriptures, but there's no mention of an altar call. Then again, we don't know if the 3,000 who were saved on the day of Pentecost came forward to some sort of "altar" or place of prayer. The problem I have with modern-day altar calls isn't the call to come forward. The problem I have is with all the trimmings that come with it—music to stir the emotions, counselors coming forward to encourage a response (and to stop the preacher from looking stupid if there's no response). Add to that the fact that many altar calls aren't calling people to repentance, but to a happier lifestyle, and it's easy to see the damage that is being done to the cause of the gospel.

Question 126

After leading people to Christ, how do you follow up with them? What tools do you give for them to develop their own personal relationship with Christ?

As I often say, our methodology will reflect our theology. I am convinced from Scripture that if someone truly comes to Christ, it is a work of God. And if he is "born of God," God will take care of him, with or without my follow-up. Phillip left the Ethiopian without follow-up. God took Phillip away from the man just after he professed faith and was baptized.

Nevertheless, I give any new converts our booklet called "Save Your-

> "No sinner looks to the Savior with a dry eye or a hard heart. Aim, therefore, at heart-breaking, at bringing home condemnation to the conscience and weaning the mind from sin."
> —CHARLES SPURGEON

self Some Pain," which contains ten principles for Christian growth. There they will find encouragement to read the Bible daily and obey it, share their faith, get into fellowship, etc. However, a genuine convert will do these things anyway. They love God's Word and feed on it, they want to be with other Christians, and they cannot help but share their faith. Understanding true and false conversion means that we don't have to be a priest (a mediator) between the professed convert and God.

To help the person find a good church, you may want to get his contact details so you can send him information about the nearest church (your church or one in his community). Then ask the pastor of that fellowship to contact the person and extend a personal invitation to his church.

Question 127

What is the difference between "follow-up" and "discipleship"?

Follow-up (in the modern sense) is when we get decisions, either through crusades or local church, and we take laborers from the harvest field, who are few as it is, and give them this disheartening task of running after these "decisions" to make sure they're continuing with God. One just has to speak to any follow-up team to know how disheartening it can be to try to get unwilling "converts" to come to church when there is no Holy Spirit driving them to do so internally. There is actually a true incident of a new "convert" being found hiding in his closet when the follow-up person came to visit.

Again, if a person is soundly saved by the Holy Spirit, it's because he was drawn by the Holy Spirit and is now indwelt by the Holy Spirit. He will *want* to know more about God and will *seek* spiritual food. *I believe in feeding a new convert. I believe in nurturing him. I believe in discipling him—that's biblical and most necessary.* But I don't believe in following him. I can't find it in Scripture.

I believe that when a person becomes a Christian, he becomes a disciple. When I bring a person to Christ through the power of the gospel, I make him a disciple. So when I preach the gospel to the unsaved and someone comes to Christ, I am "making disciples of all men."

It is common to believe that we are to get people saved, and then make "disciples" of them. But if that's the case, we have a dilemma. Is the person not a "disciple" when he surrenders to Jesus? Is Jesus not his Lord? If he isn't discipled to Him, he's not a Christian. If he is saved, but he *becomes* a disciple at a certain point in his Christian walk, who decides that point?

So, to answer the question, follow-up is running after a professed believer, while discipleship is living the normal Christian life. The message "True and False Conversion" explains this thoroughly. You can listen to it freely at www.livingwaters.com/learn/trueandfalse.htm.

Question 128

Is there ever a time when I can give someone assurance of salvation, or should I avoid it altogether?

Assurance in the believer is the job of the Holy Spirit (see Romans 8:16). However, you can point out assurance verses (Romans 10:9,10; 1 John 5:11–13, etc.), and then tell the person to appropriate faith in them.

Question 129

Why is it that you do not stress the importance of baptism? I won't add the many scriptures commanding baptism for the remission of our sins, because I am sure you already know them...just curious because I read it to be essential.

Water baptism is not essential to salvation. If you read Acts 10:44–48 carefully, you will see that the Gentiles received the Holy Spirit (they passed from death to life) before they were water baptized. Paul himself was filled with the Holy Spirit he was baptized (Acts 9:17,18). Also, the apostle Paul said that Christ sent him not to baptize, but to preach the gospel (see 1 Corinthians 1:17). It is the gospel that is the power of God to salvation, so that's what we preach. Nevertheless, it is important for the believer to obey the command to be baptized in water.

GENERAL QUESTIONS ON DOCTRINE

(How)

"If you wish to know God, you must know His Word. If you wish to perceive His power, you must see how He works by His Word. If you wish to know His purpose before it comes to pass, you can only discover it by His Word."
—CHARLES SPURGEON

Question 130

Why are there so many religions?

Mankind seems to mess up anything to which he puts his hand. He had excelled in the subject of religion. This is because idolatry knows no bounds. It's as far reaching as the imagination of man. First, you create a god, then you build a religion around it.

Question 131

How do you respond to a person who says the Bible was written by a bunch of crazy people and you have to be crazy to believe it?

I would say, "Let's not argue about the inspiration of the Bible for a moment," and then I would take him through the Commandments. Jesus didn't say, "Go into all the world and convince people that the Bible is the Word of God." It is the *gospel* that is the power of God to salvation (see Romans 1:16), and the way to give the arrow of the gospel its thrust is to put it into the bow of the Law.

We often hear that Christianity stands or falls on the validity of Scripture. I respectfully disagree. I believe the Bible is God's Word. There's no argument there. But my salvation isn't dependent upon that fact, because I wasn't converted by the Bible. I was converted by the power of God, and when I picked up a Bible it simply explained what had happened to me.

In our sincere efforts to convince a sinful world, we tend to use intellectual arguments (I'm often guilty of this) when the ultimate proof is the power of God transforming the human heart. But I didn't come to Christ through an intellectual argument, and my faith doesn't stand on human wisdom, so why should I try to bring others through that door?

If the whole scientific world came together and "disproved" the Bible, and archaeologists found what were "proved" to be the bones of Jesus, it wouldn't shake my faith in the slightest. Not at all. This is what Paul speaks about in 1 Corinthians 2:4,5 when he says that the Christian's faith doesn't rest "in the wisdom of men but in the power of God."

Remember, early Christians weren't converted by the Scriptures. Instead, they were saved by a *spoken* message. The New Testament hadn't been compiled. There was no such thing as the printing press. And most couldn't read anyway.

If you believe that our foundation for the faith is the written Scriptures rather than in the person of Jesus Christ, I have some questions for you. When did Christianity begin? Was it on the Day of Pentecost when the 3,000 were converted by the power of God, or did it have to wait until the New Testament was compiled in 200 A.D.?

So don't feel that it's your mandate to convince anyone of the inspiration of the Word of God. You will never do it while they love their sins. For every reasonable argument you come up with, he will come back with a hundred and one atrocities and injustices in the Bible.

Instead, give the arrow of the gospel thrust by using the Law of God to bring the knowledge of sin. Make the sinner thirst after righteousness, without which he will perish. Then, once he is born again and comes to know the Lord, the Scriptures will open up to him. Until that time, the things of God will seem foolishness to him, as the Scriptures say.

Question 132

I'm encountering more people who say, "Aren't morals simply the result of cultural upbringing and conditioning? We believe something is wrong just because everyone agrees it is wrong." How do you answer this?

This is called "moral relativism," and it's popular among those who don't realize that there is such a thing as moral absolutes. The unchanging standard of morality is God's Law. God is perfect, holy, just, and good, and so is His Law, because it issues from His very character. It is written in stone, and what's wrong for you is wrong for me and is wrong for every one of us. That's why it's essential to preach the Law of God. It is echoed by the conscience, and knowledge of it will cause the careless sinner to see his error.

If you ask a moral relativist if what Hitler did was *wrong*, he will say, "I would never do something like that myself, but I can't say it was *wrong*." He can't say that it was "wrong" because to him, nothing is *absolutely* right, and nothing is *absolutely* wrong. That has strong divine connotations.

So ask Mr. Relativist if pedophilia is wrong, and he will tell you that if it is against the law, it is simply wrong for *that* society. His framing of civil law is governed by whether or not people get "hurt," rather than by "right" or by "wrong." His argument will be that pedophilia hurts children. But if someone takes pictures of naked children and posts them on the Internet without their knowledge (so that it's not hurting them), then it must be morally okay. So press him. Is pedophilia morally *wrong*? If he says that it's not, ask for his name and address, because you need to inform his neighbors and the local police that he is okay with pedophilia. If he admits that it's morally wrong *even though a society says that it's right*, then so was Hitler wrong, and there are therefore moral absolutes.

Be careful that you don't get mired in pseudo intellectualism. It can be a time-waster, and you and I are told to redeem the time. You will simply win an argument, when what you should be doing is showing him that he needs God's forgiveness.

The root problem with a moral relativist is that his conscience is seared, and, with the help of God, you *must* awaken it. So, say to him, "Let's just surmise that there is a Heaven for a moment. Do you think you would be good enough to go there?" He will almost certainly say that he is (see Proverbs 20:6), so take him through the Good Person test. You are simply moving from the intellect (the place of argument), to the conscience (the place of the knowledge of right and wrong), so that it will do its God-given duty.

Question 133

When it comes to lying, are there not conditions under which it is better to lie than to tell the truth? If your wife asks you if she looks fat or if you like her dress, shouldn't you lie to protect her feelings? What about

Rahab in Joshua 2? She lied to protect the spies, then they blessed her in return by sparing her family.

This is a contentious issue. Most husbands would lie if an armed burglar asked if his wife was hiding in the house. The reason he would lie is that if he said, "Yes, she's under the bed," then he is guilty of helping him murder her. What would he say if he's forced at gunpoint to watch while the gunman rapes his wife before murdering her: "Sorry, honey; I didn't want to tell a lie"? These scenarios are often brought up by the unsaved to justify lying. But God knows the difference between incidents like these to protect the life of innocent victims, the use of "discretion" to protect someone's feelings, and bold, deceitful lies to protect ourselves.

Question 134

Isn't it unreasonable that God would judge us by our thought life?

The idea that merely thinking could be a crime does seem absurd. Absurd, that is, until you realize that if you merely conspire in your mind to kill the President of the United States, you will find yourself in serious violation of the law. Whether you express that thought verbally or in writing, you don't have to complete the act or even be actively planning it. You simply have to be thinking about it.

Some may say, "That's different. Conspiracy to murder the President is a serious crime." And that's the point. Most people don't think that sin against God is a serious crime. God does. Our moral standards are extremely low; God's are incredibly high. He is so holy, He requires perfection in thought, word, and deed. If we have hatred in our heart for another person, God sees that as murder. And if we have lustful thoughts toward another human being, God sees that as committing adultery in our heart. He judges the thoughts and intents of our heart.

Question 135

If salvation is a free gift, then why do we have to repent? It sounds like we are paying for eternal life with our repentance.

Jesus paid the price for us, so there is nothing we can ever do ourselves to earn eternal life. It is a gift that God offers to us. In fact, we are so sinful and rebellious that both the repentance and faith that we exercise are also given by God. Ephesians 2:8,9 tells us that faith is the gift of God, and 2 Timothy 2:24,25 says that repentance is "granted" to us by God. We can't even repent without God's help. Salvation is of the Lord—all of it, from beginning to end. He is the author and the finisher of our faith. Just as our first birth was a gift from God to us, so is the second birth. This may raise questions

"That sin must die, or you will perish by it. Depend on it, that sin which you would save from the slaughter will slaughter you."

—CHARLES SPURGEON

about man's free will and God's sovereignty. Conquer any questions through trust.

Question 136

What does it mean to have the righteousness of Christ?

God accounts His righteousness to us, so that we are not just prodigal sons who are forgiven but who underneath it all still smell like a pigsty. We are washed clean, clothed with a pure robe of righteousness, and given a ring of inheritance.

Question 137

How do I know if I'm saved and simply caught up in a sinful habit, or if I am in fact not saved?

Every case is different. Many Christians have a sinful habit of overeating. Others may struggle with smoking or coveting. Others have a battle with sexual sins. The big question is do they stumble into sin, or do they plan to sin? The Christian *falls* into sin; the false convert *dives* in. Some Christians believe in what is commonly called "sinless perfection" and think they can be completely without sin. I find those folks usually have a problem with a subtle form of pride, which is a big sin.

So, none of us should look down on someone who is truly struggling with their sin. The key word is "struggling." If you are doing something that you know is wrong, don't make provision for the flesh. Avoid temptation. Don't go there. Feed yourself on the Word. Cultivate the fear of God in your life. Be busy sharing your faith. Continually pray for God's help. Have an accountability partner. Try not to be alone. Keep away from boredom, because the battleground is the mind. If you have a concern for the lost, the enemy is going to target your weakness, whatever it is. Be aware of that—that your battle isn't against flesh and blood, but against demonic forces. Resist them steadfast in the faith.

Question 138

When a person has accepted the Lord as his Savior, but walks away from God and back to the things of the world, can that person return to God and be forgiven?

When someone becomes a Christian, it is more biblical to say that he *surrendered* to God, rather than that he "accepted" Him. Those who merely "accept" Christ but don't surrender to His Lordship aren't truly born again and will fall away in time (see Luke 9:62). People in this category don't "return" to God because they never knew Him in the first place. I would suggest that you listen to the message "True and False Conversion" (www.livingwaters.com/learn/trueandfalse.htm).

Question 139

What is the balance of assurance between salvation and examining oneself to see if he is in the faith?

Think of what you would do if you were wearing a parachute and waiting to jump out of a plane. You would have faith in the parachute, but you would also regularly check to make sure that the straps are firm. Once you have put on the Lord Jesus Christ through conversion (repentance and faith), you should regularly examine yourself to see how firm your relationship is with the Lord. Are you reading the Word daily? Do you have regular prayer? Are you fighting sin, or giving in to it? Are you living in holiness? Are you confessing sin? How is your relationship with other Christians? Is there any hidden bitterness against anyone? Are you sharing your faith? What is your greatest passion? Is it the Lord, or are material things more important? Do you love the world and the things in the world? On a scale of one to ten, how would you rate your walk with God? It should be a ten. If it's not, strive to make it a ten.

Question 140

I had been a professing Christian for most of my life but it wasn't until I heard the gospel through the Law in "Hell's Best Kept Secret" that I believe I was really saved. Since then, I have studied my Bible every day and I have been sharing my faith.

My question is on the teaching of election. The Bible seems to be very clearly saying that God has predestined some people to Heaven and some to Hell. He has "chosen" or "elected" to save some and not others. All who are chosen...elected...predestined...are guaranteed to hear His voice and follow Him. Those who are not—well... they'll hear the Word but will never come to repentance.

How do we reconcile these verses to the fact that "God is not willing for any to perish"? Wouldn't He then have "called" everyone *equally?* Many say that election is connected to our free will (somehow) and if we make the choice to follow Jesus, we are then "elected." But it also seems election is the *reason* we make that choice—not the *result* of the choice. Then again, God knows what choice we will make.

I know that it will not be God's fault when someone goes to Hell. It's their sin that has put them there. I have comfort in the fact that God's ways are fair but if there is any other earthly understanding to be found on this topic, I would love to find it.

I normally keep silent about this issue, but you are so earnest I wanted to share my thoughts. After over thirty years of thinking about election/predestination, etc., I find myself about where you are. I haven't figured it out, and I'm still working on it. I'm serious.

I know that God is sovereign. We don't do anything to be saved. We are saved by grace alone. But when I find myself leaning toward Calvinism, I think of a mass of verses that lean the other way. There are Bible many verses that say things to the effect that "whosoever will may come." Calvinists deal with them by adding a word here and there: "The Lord is not willing that any (of the elect) should perish but that all (of the elect) should come to repentance." "Whoever (of the elect) calls on the name of the Lord shall be saved." "God desires all men (who are the elect) to be saved and to come to the knowledge of the truth." That sends me back to the middle of the road.

Besides that, the issue is very divisive—a real church-splitter. So even if I did figure it out, I would keep it to myself for the sake of the ministry that God has entrusted me with. If I went one way or the other, doors would instantly slam.

So here is what I do to I reconcile the issue in the privacy of my own mind:

It's about 2000 B.C. You read in God's Word, "The earth hangeth upon nothing" (pre-KJV). You are instantly thrown into an intellectual dilemma. Science (and your own reason) tell you that can't be true. The earth is too heavy to "hang upon nothing." The law of gravity dictates that even a feather can't hang upon nothing.

So, you have to make a choice. Are you a "Bible-ite" or a "Reason-ite"? People are pressuring you to make a choice. What are you: Bible-ite or Reason-ite?

But you don't have to go one way or the other. You decide to stay in the middle, trusting God, and waiting about 4,000 years for some missing information.

It comes in 1800 A.D., when science discovers that there is no gravity in space. That missing information shows you how the earth (though it weighs multiple octillions of tons) can freely float in space, lighter than a feather.

So the question arises: What are you? Are you a Calvinist or are you an Armenianist? You have to side with one or the other. Which camp are you in? Don't be a theological wimp. One way or the other.

133

But you don't have to go one way or the other. Simply decide to stay in the middle, trusting God, and then patiently wait for some missing information.

The day will come when we know all things (see 1 Corinthians 13:12), and when that time comes and I suddenly understand how it was that two opposing thoughts could both be true, I will be glad that I didn't spend hours arguing with my brethren and causing division in the Body of Christ. It is then that I will be truly glad that I instead put my time and energy into reaching out to the lost.

Question 141

Where do you stand on the body of Christ having different functions? In the Bible, the body of Christ is paralleled to our human body. All of us should be representatives of the Body and should always be prepared to witness where called to do so. However, I think that some are to be planters and some should feed, some harvest, and some glean. Do you believe that if I am gleaning, picking up those who fall, that I am not doing what I am called to do? I love sharing the Lord with people and do so often, but I have learned that God has a specific place and function for me and that is where I focus my energies. It seems you believe that if everyone is not out there doing "your method" of evangelism then perhaps they are not even saved.

The main parallel to the human body is in 1 Corinthians 12:14–31. Each part has its own function. That's a healthy body. But notice in that passage, the parallel is in-reach (within the local church), not outreach (evangelism):

"And God has appointed these in the church: first apostles, second prophets, third teachers, etc." (verse 28).

There is no mention of evangelists in that portion of Scripture because it's in the context of the Church coming together, and when all those functions are working well, we have a healthy Church. Then, when the Church is healthy, it will (as one body) do what it has been commanded to do by the Head: to reach out to the lost.

We are like survivors in a lifeboat of the *Titanic*. All around us are drowning people. We need every hand onboard to help reach those who are dying and pull them into the boat. We think and move as one mind and one body. Nothing else matters. Love is our motivation. Every hand is needed—because there is a terrible lack of rescuers. Why? Because some think that their job is to sit in the lifeboat, and, knowing that people are perishing, busy themselves polishing the brass.

If that's the case, one has to question if they are really part of the body, because the Head has commanded us to reach out to those who are perishing (Mark 16:15). A hand that doesn't do what the Head commands it to isn't healthy.

I'm not concerned what "method" people use to reach out, as long as they are doing it the way the Bible tells us to. Otherwise, they are just pulling corpses into the boat, and we see the fruit of that within the contemporary Church.

Question 142

In your analogy about pulling people into the lifeboat, perhaps not all of the people behind you are polishing brass. Some people (prayer support) are holding onto your belt to keep you from falling back into the icy water, and others (those who minister to new believers) are wrapping those icy victims in blankets, giving them soup, etc. Are the people doing the other jobs "not saved" because they aren't leaning out all the time and pulling people into the boat?

I appreciate what you are saying. But our problem is that 98% of the professed Body of Christ in America *are* praying and ministering to new believers. Only 2% are reaching out to the unsaved. So, let's put it another way. Imagine that a number of little children sneak out of a house, get into a rubber raft in a swimming pool, and it overturns. Their parents hear them scream, rush outside and see that the kids are drowning. Each of the adults can swim but instead of jumping in to save the children, they stand back and let one man try to save all the children. At the court hearing on the deaths of five of the kids, the defense of those who stood back was that they saw their job as being one of getting warm towels and dry clothing ready for the children, for when they were rescued. The judge would be horrified at their defense and say that their *real* motive was that they did not want to get cold and wet. He would no doubt say that the blood of those dead children was on their guilty hands, and give each of them stiff prison terms.

Every Christian has been told to do more than stand back and pray. We have been *commanded* to jump into the waters of personal evangelism (see Matthew 28:19,20; Mark 16:15; 2 Corinthians 5:19,20; etc.). Yet most choose to do *everything but* what we have been commanded to do. Personally, I would rather stand back and let other people reach out to the lost, but I can't. How could I say that the love of God dwells in me if I let people perish, simply because I was concerned about my own comfort and well-being? Love could never do that. If I stood back and busied myself with other things, I then cannot have assurance (biblically) that I had passed from death to life. That's why Charles Spurgeon said, "Have you no wish for others to be saved? Then you are not saved yourself, be sure of that."

But the lack of laborers isn't the problem. That's just the symptom. The problem is that we have millions of false converts sitting in the Church. They have cold hearts and don't love their neighbor as much as they love themselves. But when someone is truly born again, the love of Christ "constrains" them. They immediately reach out to the unsaved. The will of God to seek the lost becomes their number one priority. And how could it not, with so many perishing around us?

Question 143

Can you explain why Christians worship on Sunday instead of keeping the Sabbath?

We keep the first day of the week because that's what the disciples did. There is no command anywhere in the New Testament for Christians to keep the Jewish Sabbath. In fact, the Scriptures say we should not to let any man tell us what day to keep. Seventh Day Adventists are welcome to keep the Sabbath, but they shouldn't attempt to tell others to do as they do. If they had half as much zeal for the lost as they do for telling Christians what day to rest, we would have revival.

Question 144

Why did God tell Joshua to kill men, women, and children?

[I will let Mark Spence, the Dean of the School of Biblical Evangelism, answer this one:] The reason we can so quickly fault God for wiping out multitudes of people is that we have a subjective definition of what is "good."

For example, we define *good* perhaps as helping some old lady across the street. Someone watching us do such a task is impressed with our servanthood and gives us kudos. However, we don't see the big picture. If we knew that sweet old lady whom we just helped was crossing that street to slip cyanide in everyone's cups at the corner coffee shop, we hopefully wouldn't have helped her carry out the task.

Or we may think it is a *good* task to give money to someone on the street. While that may *seem* noble, what if you discovered that the person was going to use it to purchase drugs? It would not be such a *good* thing after all, would it?

Or we may think it is *good* to give a stranger a ride to the grocery store. While that act may *seem* noble, what if you discovered that the person was going there to rob the joint? It would not be such a *good* thing after all, would it?

"Avoid a sugared gospel as you would shun sugar of lead. Seek that gospel which rips up and tears and cuts and wounds and hacks and even kills, for that is the gospel that makes alive again."
—CHARLES SPURGEON

Therefore, who among you is able to define good? What gives you the right to say what God does is right or wrong? If goodness is subjective, then there is no right or wrong. Rather, you could only say that what God did is not your preference. However, even then, how can you make that statement since you are not omniscient to know whether destroying a certain people group was the correct action based on all the information?

Therefore, God alone has the right to define what is *good*. With God seeing the whole picture, He never makes a mistake. There is no hindsight with God. Everything God does is motivated by His nature: His goodness, His justice, His holiness. And that is why God can kill an individual or a group of people, like the Amalekites, and it can be a good thing. In fact, it can be considered the best thing.

Rather than standing in judgment over God, when we have all the information, we discover that God is justified in killing not only the Amalekites, but all of us. We all are sentenced to die because we have broken His holy Law a multitude of times. But God, in His love, paid the penalty for our sin so we wouldn't have to die.

CLOSING
THOUGHTS

G od bless you for your concern for the lost, and for your concern that we reach out to them biblically. Never lose sight of what God is using you for. He has trusted you with the message of *everlasting life*. Never forget that you have an enemy, and perhaps his greatest weapon is discouragement. If you want to reach the lost and you particularly want to preach open-air, be ready for attacks. Be ready for fear. Be ready for discouragement to come from the least expected places. It will often come from Christian friends or family who will tell you that you are unloving or overboard. Being shot by your own side is called "friendly fire," but there's nothing "friendly" about it. It's worse than being shot from in front. So keep your shield of faith held high. Make sure you are soaked in the love of God. Be resolute. Be faithful.

Here's a prayer of resolution:

"Father, I thank you for the shed blood of Jesus. It is because of His blood that I can boldly come before Your throne. Please help me to always remember that You have trusted me with the message of salvation for this lost and dying world. Let Your love be my motivation. Help me never to be discouraged, distracted, or disillusioned. Help me to keep my heart free from sin, and to always keep my eyes on Jesus, the author and finisher of our faith. Help me to always speak and preach knowing that You are listening to my every word, and may I always be a true and faithful witness. In Jesus' precious name I pray. Amen."

"We must school and train ourselves to deal personally with the unconverted. We must not excuse ourselves, but force ourselves to the irksome task until it becomes easy."

—CHARLES SPURGEON

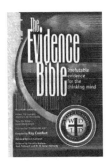

The Evidence Bible

"*The Evidence Bible* is specially designed to reinforce the faith of our times by offering hard evidence and scientific proof for the thinking mind."

—Dr. D. James Kennedy

The Evidence Bible, based on more than two decades of research, has been commended by Josh McDowell, Franklin Graham, Dr. Woodrow Kroll, and many other Christian leaders.

- Learn how to show the absurdity of evolution.

- See from Scripture how to prove God's existence without the use of faith.

- Discover how to prove the authenticity of the Bible through prophecy.

- See how the Bible is full of eye-opening scientific and medical facts.

- Read fascinating quotes from Darwin, Einstein, Newton, and other well-known scientists.

- Learn how to share your faith with your family, neighbors, and coworkers, as well as Muslims, Mormons, Jehovah's Witnesses, etc.

- Glean evangelistic wisdom from Charles Spurgeon, John Wesley, George Whitefield, D. L. Moody, John MacArthur, and many others.

- Discover answers to 100 common objections to Christianity.

Find out how to answer questions such as: Where did Cain get his wife? Why is there suffering? Why are there "contradictions" in the Bible?...and much more!

School of Biblical Evangelism

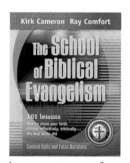

Do you want to deepen your passion for the lost, for the cross, and for God? Then look no further. Join more than 10,000 students from around the world in the School of Biblical Evangelism, to learn how to witness and defend the faith.

With 101 lessons on subjects ranging from basic Christian doctrines to knowing our enemy, from false conversions to proving the deity of Jesus, you will be well-equipped to answer questions as you witness to anyone. This study course will help you to prove the authenticity of the Bible, provide ample evidence for creation, refute the claims of evolution, understand the beliefs of those in cults and other religions, and know how to reach both friends and strangers with the gospel.

"A phenomenal course."
—Jim Culver

*"Awesome... This course should be required
in every theological seminary."*
—Spencer S. Hanley

*"As a graduate of every other evangelism course I can find,
yours by far has been the best."*
—Bill Lawson

*"I have never seen anything as powerful as the
teaching in the School of Biblical Evangelism."*
—James W. Smith

Join online at **www.biblicalevangelism.com**
or, to obtain the entire course in book form,
call **800-437-1893** or visit fine bookstores everywhere